Here We Are in
BIBLE LANDS
With
JOHN R. RICE

Here We Are in

BIBLE LANDS

With

JOHN R. RICE

By

Dr. John R. Rice

SWORD OF THE LORD PUBLISHERS
Murfreesboro, Tennessee 37130

ISBN 0-87398-375-0 (hard binding)
ISBN 0-87398-376-9 (paper binding)

Printed and Bound in the United States of America

AAQ-2595   AA0-0476

Table of Contents

List of Illustrations

Introduction

Every sincere attempt to illustrate the Word of God is commendable. Commentaries are daily rolling off the presses; travelogs are innumerable; sermon books are without number, as many today, making pilgrimages to Bible lands, come back to tell about it. All these aid the Bible student in seeking more light on Scripture.

For fifteen years Dr. John R. Rice has spent from fifteen to twenty-one days a year walking where Jesus walked. He has resided amid the scenes and the scenery. From early morning to late at night he has gazed upon them with an enthusiasm that never tired.

Of course, we know, to describe these things, one must have seen and *felt* them; this the author has done through his many years of adventure; so he is thoroughly competent to write about them.

And one of the reasons for the popularity of Dr. Rice's Sword Tours has been Dr. Rice himself and his nightly briefings on the places to be seen the next day or the next. And his knowledge of the Bible is far beyond that of the guides and of most tour directors, so that makes his description of the places discussed more vivid and rich.

But why limit his knowledge to just the hundreds who hear him in person as they journeyed with him? Why not let the thousands profit also?

So he was persuaded upon his return in 1976 to "sermonize" what he actually saw as he conducted his tours through Jerusalem and some of the most celebrated localities in its neighborhood.

Most of my life has been spent under the ministry of my boss, Dr. John R. Rice. And he is the kind of Christian who does one good just to be with, and to work for. The simplicity of his life, the contagion of his enthusiasm, the fullness of his surrender, and the depth of his devotion to Christ hearten everyone who knows him. The Lord is as real to him as those who live and work with him—if anything, more real. And you will find yourself in these sermons walking with him over the golden streets of Holy Jerusalem!

It was my privilege to be with Dr. Rice on twelve tours of the Holy Land. Time and time again I have heard some Sword tour member say that his talks, the tour itself, was much like a spiritual revival. Hundreds have been saved on our tours. Sometimes it has been a guide or a tour agent or an Arab hungry for someone to show him the way to Jesus.

We sincerely pray that you will find this an interesting and informative book on the land made forever sacred because our Lord and His apostles lived there. Dr. Rice's descriptions of the places put in sermon form are different but definitely fresh. Read these chapters with open mind and heart, and you will be richly blessed; you will gain fresh knowledge of the places Dr. Rice discusses therein.

Viola Walden

January, 1977

Foreword

Considerably more than one thousand people have gone with me on fourteen tours of the Holy Land. Day after day and night after night, over there, I have taught them the things I am teaching and preaching here. How God has blessed us!

In the small Mamertine dungeon at Rome where Paul, in his second imprisonment, wrote to Timothy, his farewell message, saying, "I am now ready to be offered, and the time of my departure is at hand," we gather. As we read Paul's words urging Timothy to come before winter and to bring the cloke, we wonder if Timothy got there before Paul was beheaded. And we rejoice that God had somebody like Paul to pay the price of martyrdom and win souls at any cost. Then each time we have sung

> **"Faith of our fathers! living still**
> **In spite of dungeon, fire, and sword,"**

and had a prayer of dedication.

We will never forget some of those times when we stood by the Sea of Galilee where Jesus called Peter, Andrew, James and John to be fishers of men. Or when we stood at the ruins of the old synagogue in Capernaum and recounted how God saved and healed the man let down through the roof by his four faithful friends, how He healed the withered hand in the synagogue.

People have climbed with me that solid stone Mount, Mars' Hill, half way up the Acropolis in Athens. We recounted Paul's sermon there about "the unknown god." They went with me out to the ruins of old Corinth, sixty miles west, and we stood at was the "Bema," the judgment seat, before which Paul was brought and acquitted.

This year there were a good many tears as we stood on Mount Nebo in the mountains of Moab and looked, as Moses did, across the Jordan River valley to see all over the Promised Land. We remembered how Moses laid down his burdens, bade the people farewell, and there was buried in a secret grave by the hand of God.

Again and again we have gone to the Garden of Gethsemane. And many times they would let us go out under those eight ancient olive trees to kneel and have our devotions. Always we remind the people of the Saviour there with the bloody sweat, the traitor's kiss, His betrayal by Judas.

The crowning time has often been when we went to Joseph's new tomb and each one with a little time of devotion in that tomb, then we met for a service, remembering the burial and resurrection of Jesus and the wonderful things that followed. Oh, we will never forget those times!

I want thousands of you to go with me in these messages from my heart, to the Holy Land, and thus find real and precious the places, the people, the events associated with them.

We have had many saved in these trips to the Holy Land. Once when we stopped in Beirut in Lebanon, I was invited to speak to a private high school. The pupils were Arabs. Some were from Greek Catholic families, some Armenian, some Druses, some Moslem and other groups. We had fifty-two claim Christ as Saviour in that high school. Each one was carefully dealt with.

In old Jerusalem, in the Arab high school, there were fourteen senior boys; five of them we saw come to Christ, and, oh, how happily they followed us about to learn what they could! One of them now has already taken training in America to preach the Gospel.

We had three brothers in a bazzar in Jerusalem turn happily to Christ, and we have seen them again and again. Their sister, a schoolteacher, came down and Mrs. Rice led her to the Lord.

It was a joy to lead a lovely, cultured woman, perhaps thirty, an ardent Greek Catholic, to the Lord on the island of Cyprus.

A woman in a Lutheran church in Wisconsin got a burden to be saved but she did not know how. She wondered if she could get saved if she went to the Holy Land. A Catholic woman where she worked was a subscriber to THE SWORD OF THE LORD and she said to her friend, "Dr. John Rice takes a big group to the Holy Land every year. You should go with him." So she reserved a place and went with us. In Jerusalem one of our men preached a simple gospel sermon. She trusted Christ and was wonderfully saved! How she rejoiced in knowing her sins were forgiven! She came to say to me, "Jesus said seek and ye shall find, and I sought and I found!"

This year it was a joy to win an Arab guide, a university graduate, a sensible, modest man, to the Lord. Afterward he said to me, "For a long time I have wanted to learn more about this." And this year as we sang and gave testimonies while traveling in one of our three buses, a woman, who had asked us to pray for her, suddenly came forward and said, "I have now been saved. I have now trusted Christ." It was like a revival day after day!

I want God to make this book a blessing. So let us go together into the Bible lands and into the great events of the Scriptures we will tell about, and most of all, let us learn more about Jesus!

1977

John R. Rice

I. Rome: Paul in Mamertine Dungeon; Peter Never in Rome

In fourteen tours of Bible lands, we have always stopped at Rome. Rome was for so long the head of the world government, and, for many centuries, the head of the Catholic religion. It has so many relics, sculptures, buildings, paintings of the culture of the world. And there is St. Peters, the Mamertine Prison, the Colosseum, The Church of the Holy Stairs, the Church of St. Paul-Outside-the-Walls and the Catacombs. The truth is, Paul himself came to Rome and here he was martyred. Aside from human tradition that abounds about St. Peter and Rome, there is much to interest a cultivated man, particularly a Christian.

St. Peters is the largest church building or "Basilica" in the world, being nearly 700 feet long. The giant dome is 450 feet high, designed by Michelangelo shortly before his death.

St. Peters adjoins the Vatican Palace, home of the pope; Vatican Museum, the Sistine Chapel, etc. All is part of Vatican City, an independent state, not a part of the Italian country but enclosed in Italy. The Vatican has its own government, its own postal service and stamps, its own police, who are the famous Swiss Guards, wearing the colorful uniform, designed, it is said, by Michelangelo himself.

In front of St. Peters is the great St. Peters Square, actually more a circle than a square. Here great crowds gather. On certain days a window in the pope's apartment, facing this square, opens and the pope appears to bless the people and sometimes to address them.

St. Peters

In that giant building, not an auditorium as are our church buildings, are a number of open chapels where sometimes Masses are said or babies are sprinkled. There is the beautiful statue of The Pieta by Michelangelo, marble sculpture picturing Mary holding the dead Christ in her arms. There is also a metal statue representing Peter, with his big toe much worn by the touches of those who rub it as they come to worship and sometimes kiss it.

This giant church building is the center and worldwide symbol of the papacy and of the Catholic religion. That religion is based, to begin with, on a misinterpretation of two or three passages of Scripture and then on a world of human unreliable tradition, usually manufactured, not true to the Bible but believed by prejudiced people and it bolsters the hold of Rome and the priesthood on the masses of people.

But the Catholic religion, centering in Rome, is a religion of tradition, which makes of none effect the Word of God. Jesus talked about that here:

"He answered and said unto them, Well hath Esaias prophesied of you hypocrites, as it is written, This people honoureth me with their lips, but their heart is far from me. Howbeit in vain do they worship me, teaching for doctrines the commandments of men. For laying aside the commandment of God, ye hold the tradition of men, as the washing of pots and cups: and many other such like things ye do. And he said unto them, Full well ye reject the commandment of God, that ye may keep your own tradition. For Moses said, Honour thy father and thy mother; and, Whoso curseth father or mother, let him die the death: But ye say, If a man shall say to his father or mother, It is Corban, that is to say, a gift, by whatsoever thou mightest be profited by me; he shall be free. And ye suffer him no more to do ought for his father or his mother; Making the word of God of none effect through your tradition, which ye have delivered: and many such like things do ye."—Mark 7:6-13.

I. SCRIPTURES WHICH ARE THE MISINTERPRETED FOUNDATION OF CATHOLICISM

All over the world, Roman Catholicism is subject to the pope. But Greece, Russia, the Armenians, the Syrians, the Copts and the Philippines have independent Catholic churches, with archbishops who are not subject to the pope but still largely built on the same kind of tradition with priests, Masses, etc.

1. The Church Is Not Built Upon the Apostle Peter

Matthew 16:16-18 is misinterpreted by Rome, and that misinterpretation is absolutely essential if there be a Catholic Church, a Catholic religion.

"And Simon Peter answered and said, Thou art the Christ, the Son of the living God. And Jesus answered and said unto him,

Blessed art thou, Simon Bar-jona: for flesh and blood hath not revealed it unto thee, but my Father which is in heaven. And I say also unto thee, That thou art Peter, and upon this rock I will build my church; and the gates of hell shall not prevail against it."

Verse 18 is a play on words. Jesus said, "Thou art Peter," and the word for Peter is *Petros,* literally, "a little rock." Jesus said, "And upon this rock [*Petra*] I will build my church." He does not promise to build His church upon Peter but on Himself, as Peter is careful to tell us in I Peter 2:4-6. Peter is "the little rock"; but on Christ, "the Bedrock," the church is built. That is the clear meaning of this Scripture in the Greek New Testament. And on Himself, "the Bedrock," Christ will build His church.

First Peter 2:4-8 tells us:

"To whom coming, as unto a living stone, disallowed indeed of men, but chosen of God, and precious, Ye also, as lively stones, are built up a spiritual house, an holy priesthood, to offer up spiritual sacrifices, acceptable to God by Jesus Christ. Wherefore also it is contained in the scripture, Behold, I lay in Sion a chief corner stone, elect, precious: and he that believeth on him shall not be confounded. Unto you therefore which believe he is precious: but unto them which be disobedient, the stone which the builders disallowed, the same is made the head of the corner, And a stone of stumbling, and a rock of offence, even to them which stumble at the word, being disobedient: whereunto also they were appointed."

Christ is "a living stone" and we "as lively stones, are built up a spiritual house" on Christ. And Christ is "the Bedrock," He is "the corner stone" (vs. 6), He is "a stone of stumbling" (vs. 8).

Is the church, then, built on Peter? No. In I Corinthians 3:10-12 Paul was inspired to write to the Corinthians:

"According to the grace of God which is given unto me, as a wise masterbuilder, I have laid the foundation, and another buildeth thereon. But let every man take heed how he buildeth thereupon. For other foundation can no man lay than that is laid, which is Jesus Christ. Now if any man build upon this foun-

dation gold, silver, precious stones, wood, hay, stubble. . . ."

Will you note that one who is saved is built on Christ. And "other foundation can no man lay than that is laid, which is Jesus Christ." Nobody else can be the foundation on which souls are saved or on which the church is built, but Jesus.

2. Peter Did Not Have Power to Forgive Sins or Save One

But note again Matthew 16:19. The Lord said, "I will give unto thee the keys of the kingdom of heaven: and whatsoever thou shalt bind on earth shall be bound in heaven: and whatsoever thou shalt loose on earth shall be loosed in heaven."

Dr. Scofield says:

> Not the keys of the church, but of the kingdom of heaven in the sense of Mt. 13., i.e. the sphere of Christian profession. A key is a badge of power or authority (cf. Isa. 22. 22; Rev. 3.7). The apostolic history explains and limits this trust, for it was Peter who opened the door of Christian opportunity to Israel on the day of Pentecost (Acts 2. 38-42), and to Gentiles in the house of Cornelius (Acts 10. 34-46). There was no assumption by Peter of any other authority (Acts 15. 7-11). In the council James, not Peter, seems to have presided (Acts 15. 19; cf. Gal. 2. 11-15). Peter claimed no more for himself than to be an apostle by gift (1 Pet. 1.1), and an elder by office (1 Pet. 5.1).

Did Jesus mean that Peter could save or damn people? That he had the power to forgive sins and make people Christians? Not at all. Peter never claimed it; the Bible denies it. This same statement as in Matthew 16:19, was made again in John 20:19-23, the day Jesus arose from the dead:

"Then the same day at evening, being the first day of the week, when the doors were shut where the disciples were assembled for fear of the Jews, came Jesus and stood in the midst, and saith unto them, Peace be unto you. And when he had so said, he shewed unto them his hands and his side. Then were the disciples glad, when they saw the Lord. Then said Jesus to them again, Peace be unto you: as my Father hath sent me, even so send I you. And when he had said this, he breathed on them, and saith unto them, Receive ye the Holy Ghost: Whose soever sins

ye remit, they are remitted unto them; and whose soever sins ye retain, they are retained."

It is clear here that whatever the Lord Jesus meant in Matthew 16:19 He means here, not just for Peter but for all the apostles. Whose soever sins they remitted, they were remitted unto them; and whose soever sins they retained they are retained.

But the simple truth is, as a great Greek scholar called to my attention, that could be translated, "Whose soever sins ye remit, they shall have been remitted unto them; and whose soever sins ye retain, they shall have been retained." But in any case it is quite clear that any Christian who is filled with the Spirit and knows that one has trusted Christ for salvation has a right to say to him that his sins are remitted. And when a Christian knows that a sinner rejects Christ and has never trusted Him for salvation, he has a right to say that he is unforgiven, his sins are retained.

Not only was this same teaching to all the apostles, but the apostles were commanded in the Great Commission that when people were saved under their preaching they should give the same commission, the same commands, the same instruction to them as they themselves had received: we are to get people saved just as the apostles did. See Matthew 28:19,20 which says:

"Go ye therefore, and teach all nations, baptizing them in the name of the Father, and of the Son, and of the Holy Ghost: Teaching them to observe all things whatsoever I have commanded you: and, lo, I am with you alway, even unto the end of the world. Amen."

When one is saved, he should be baptized, then he should be taught to observe exactly what the Lord Jesus commanded the apostles.

It simply comes down to this: The Bible has such a clear plan of salvation so often stated that it is not only foolish but wicked to present another plan of salvation. In John 3:16 is the sweet promise, "For God so loved the world, that he gave his only begotten Son, that whosoever believeth in him should not perish, but have everlasting life." One who believes in Christ, one who puts his trust in Him, relies on Him for salvation "shall not perish, but have everlasting life." And that statement is repeated in John 1:12; John 3:15, 18, 36; John 5:24; John 6:40,47. Peter himself repeats it in Acts 10:43; Acts 13:38,39. Paul said it in Acts 16:31. For anyone to teach that there is some other plan of salvation aside from penitent trust in Christ, is presumption, a false gospel which denies that all who trust in Christ for salvation are saved.

So we must insist, as the Apostle Peter did in Acts 4:12, "Neither is there salvation in any other: for there is none other

Colosseum

name under heaven given among men, whereby we must be saved" but the name of Jesus.

You can see, then, that traditions of Rome have made of none effect the clear statements of the Bible. They presented, then, a false plan of salvation, salvation through the church and priesthood instead of through Jesus Christ Himself.

3. The Sacrifice of the Mass Is Sacrilegious, Dishonors Christ

But since Rome has taken on the pope and the priesthood to forgive sins and get people into Heaven or keep them out of Heaven, then they felt they must have some saving sacrifices. And so they have made the tradition that when the host is elevated, that is, when the bread and wine of the communion, or the Eucharist, are presented, they actually become the body and the blood of Christ. Thus Christ is offered again and again as a bloody sacrifice and with saving merit. There is no teaching in the Bible like that.

But when Jesus died on the cross, He said boldly, "It is finished." Then the plan of salvation is finished, and the atonement for sin is finished.

Ah, and the Bible teaching is clear that when one takes Christ as Saviour, relying on Him, receiving Him by faith as Saviour, then his sins are all forgiven and there can be no more offering for sins. Hebrews 10:16-18 says:

"This is the covenant that I will make with them after those days, saith the Lord, I will put my laws into their hearts, and in their minds will I write them; And their sins and iniquities will I remember no more. Now where remission of these is, there is no more offering for sin."

Here we find a horrible result of going by tradition instead of by the Bible. We have a false plan of salvation, salvation by a system or a human priesthood, salvation by men instead of salvation by God. That necessarily involves a false gospel that cannot save. It involves the curse of Galatians 1:8,9:

"But though we, or an angel from heaven, preach any other gospel unto you than that which we have preached unto you, let him be accursed. As we said before, so say I now again, If any

*man preach any other gospel unto you than that ye have
received, let him be accursed."*

II. THE ROMAN TRADITION HIDES THE GOSPEL
FROM MILLIONS

While we are here in Rome and speak of the traditions of
Rome, let us consider with deep concern of soul that Roman
tradition and the teachings of many churches and religions hide
the Gospel. It is overlaid with traditions that keep multitudes
away from Christ and salvation. As Jesus said to the Pharisees,
these leaders are "making the word of God of none effect through
your tradition" (Mark 7:13).

It is shocking to see that Romish tradition has made the plan
of salvation hidden from the most ardent Catholics.

God's plan of salvation is simple. All are sinners and need to be
born again and have changed hearts. But Christ died and atoned
for all our sins. That atonement was finished on the cross; there
is to be no more sacrifice for sin, no more payments for sin.
Forgiveness, salvation is the free gift of God.

One who trusts in Christ to forgive and save him immediately
has everlasting life. So say John 3:16 and many other Scriptures.
One who turns from sin to trust in Christ is already saved
without the Mass, without confession to a priest, without any
rite, any ceremony of the church.

But the truth is, multitudes of good Catholics have never been
converted, have never committed their souls once for all to
Christ for forgiveness and salvation. So good Catholics generally
have no assurance that they are saved, that they will get to
Heaven. A Catholic priest does not have that assurance. The
Catholic bishop, the archbishop, the cardinal do not know that
they are saved, for Catholic dogma teaches that no one is saved
for sure but the saints who have had miracles. And saints are
only recognized and canonized long after they are dead!

Surely some Catholics in their hearts turn to Christ for salvation and find it. Through all the darkness of tradition that hides
the Gospel, many trust Christ and are saved. But they usually
are not sure of it. I am glad that no one who comes to Christ is

turned down. But we have found that most Catholics have never heard the Gospel, have never been born again, though they do claim they have been. As Paul said about Jews (and it is true about many Protestants and Catholics), "For they being ignorant of God's righteousness, and going about to establish their own righteousness, have not submitted themselves unto the righteousness of God" (Rom. 10:3).

1. "We Had the Wrong Priest, That Is Why We Had No Peace"

I was in revival services at Lake Arthur, Louisiana, among the French Acadian Catholics. Nearly all spoke French and did not speak English. Down the Mermentau River I went with the pastor and a Christian Acadian. We saw a man and his sixteen-year-old son beside a great gum tree they had cut down. They talked to him about the Gospel in French. I understand only a little French. His eyes burned so, I felt I must help. So I touched him on the shoulder and looked him in the face and said, "You need no priest but Jesus!"

He looked at me with some astonishment. I said it again, "You need no priest but Jesus!"

He understood a little English. He began to speak rapidly in French and his face was all excited. They told me what he said: "Ah, I know now why I never had any peace. I prayed, I went to Mass, I confessed to the priest, I did all I knew, but never had any peace. I see it now! I had the wrong priest! And I take Jesus to be my Priest."

I was astonished at his quick reaction. Could one with only such Gospel as he knew be saved so immediately? Then I remembered he knew about the death of Christ on the cross. He had only missed the truth that he could personally take Christ as his Saviour, rely on Him and have it settled forever. And now he did that.

I saw him and his wife and that son come that night in the services. They all three came forward and claimed the Lord openly. Each one witnessed and someone interpreted to me that they had just learned that day that they could have Christ as their High Priest forever, that He paid everything, that was all they needed and they had trusted Him! I saw the three of them baptized in beautiful Lake Arthur!

Oh, Catholics everywhere need to know they need "no priest but Jesus."

2. "My Religion Might Be Good Enough to Live by but It Would Not Do to Die by"

So said a distraught young woman to me in a tent revival campaign at Dill, Oklahoma, years ago.

The young lady had sat with deepest attention and concern on her face. At the invitation she came to speak to me earnestly. She told me how she had been a practicing Catholic, attended Mass, prayed to Mary, confessed to a priest, had been confirmed. But then she became sick. Her condition worsened and worsened until she lay at death's door. A horrible fear possessed her. She dared not go out to meet God knowing she was a poor, unforgiven sinner. All she depended on seemed to fade away.

So she told me, "I promised God that if He would let me live, I would find out what the real way of salvation was. I told the Lord, 'I have to have something fit to die by. I will go to any length to find what You want me to do to be saved.' "

She got well. So when the big tent was erected and the services advertised, she came with a seeking heart. She said to me now, "I have to know for sure. What I have might be good enough to live by, but it won't do to die by." Oh, she got assurance when she put her trust in Christ and knew her sins were forgiven!

I saw her earnestly warn her younger sister, "You must make sure, you must be sure that your trust is in Jesus and know your sins are forgiven."

Ah, millions have some hope, but they are relying on their own righteousness, or on the church ceremonies, or on the church, or the priest, or preacher, or on a good life. They go about to establish their own righteousness but have not submitted themselves to the righteousness of Christ. Oh, how sad when tradition covers up the Gospel!

3. "You Are Right. I Hated to Believe It but I Must!"

I had a letter from Nova Scotia from a woman who had read

my article in THE SWORD, "What Is Wrong With the Roman Church?" It was written kindly but clearly and scripturally. Some woman left THE SWORD OF THE LORD on her porch and she wrote:

> I didn't want to believe it, but I must. You are right. The pope is not God on earth. The Bible doesn't say you should pray to Mary. It doesn't teach that a priest can forgive sins. A priest was coming to my house tomorrow, but I have sent word for him not to come. I am renouncing my Roman religion and today am trusting Christ to be my own Saviour. This is all so new to me, Dr. Rice, you must pray for me.

In the same issue of THE SWORD OF THE LORD was a sermon to the unsaved, making clear strongly the plan of salvation. She signed the decision form claiming Christ and sent a year's subscription to THE SWORD.

Oh, let nothing cover the sweet Gospel, that one who trusts in Christ now for forgiveness and salvation is born again; he has everlasting life; he has a home in Heaven.

III. MANY TRADITIONS MADE TO ORDER IN ROME ABOUT PETER

1. It is now said that they have found the bones of the Apostle Peter buried under the Church of St. Peters. It was only a few years ago that they claimed to find these bones. So that is a new tradition.

However, here is a shocking sidelight on it. Fifteen years ago I was in Rome, before this tradition was founded, before the papacy announced the bones of Peter had been found buried under St Peters Church. And fifteen years ago a priest, running the booth in the Church of the Holy Stairs, sold me a booklet about the Church of St. John Lateran which is known as the home church of the pope, and this booklet said that St. John Lateran Church had had, since the twelfth century, I believe, "the bones of St. Peter and St. Paul" and kept these treasured relics!

Now they have found the bones of St. Peter again buried under the church at Rome. Were there two Peters? I inquired for a copy of that booklet in Rome afterward, and it was no longer on sale. They had stopped claiming that they had the bones of Peter and

Saluti da ROMA

The Holy Stairs

Paul at the Church of St. John Lateran. The pamphlet, *The Cathedral of the Pope*, a description of the Church of St. John the Lateran by J. B. de Toth, page 20, tells of a mosaic there which pictures "the two Princes of the Apostles, Peter and Paul,—an allusion to Rome and the Lateran, where their heads are preserved." Now the old one was a tradition which was not true; the new one is also a tradition and not true. And it goes to show how they manufacture legends and traditions to keep the affections and devotion of the common people.

2. I often go to the Mamertine Prison over which a Catholic church has been built. That prison seems to have been the death house under the palace of the Caesars or in that vicinity. And we have some reason to believe that it was there that Paul the apostle came in a second imprisonment and that there he prepared to die and wrote II Timothy where he said:

"For I am now ready to be offered, and the time of my departure is at hand. I have fought a good fight, I have finished my course, I have kept the faith: Henceforth there is laid up for me a crown of righteousness, which the Lord, the righteous judge, shall give me at that day: and not to me only, but unto all them also that love his appearing."—II Tim. 4:6-8.

It is a heart-moving thing to go down into that dungeon where for long years the only entrance was that round hole in the top where a man could be let down into the prison and where food could be let down. Now a stairway has been built for tourists. Catholics say this was the prison of Paul *and Peter*, with more emphasis on Peter. In fact, a big bronze medallion on the wall celebrates the tradition that Simon Peter was there and when he wanted to baptize a person, a spring miraculously broke out in the floor of this dungeon; and there is the picture of Peter sprinkling a fellow! Now the truth is, Peter was never at Rome. And if Peter had been in Rome, he would not have sprinkled people, because the Roman Catholic Church did not change baptism by immersion to sprinkling until the twelfth and thirteenth centuries. Nobody ever heard of sprinkling as baptism, even among Catholics, until that time. Even the old Catholic Church at Nazareth had a baptistry. The ruins of the Church of St. John at

Ephesus had a pit for baptizing by immersion which I saw. But to strengthen the Roman papacy, Catholics determined to have Peter in Rome!

And traditions grow rapidly. Some years ago as I went down into this dungeon—the Mamertine Prison—cemented on the wall by the stairway was a bit of marble that looked like it had received a blow. The surface was fractured and cracked. Beside it was a legend saying that here Peter, when he was arrested, struck his head and left this fracture on the marble! That had not been there when I visited the prison several years before! The next year when I went back, it was removed! It was obviously too bald an imposition to be believed.

3. At the Church of St. Paul-Outside-the-Walls, traditionally built near where Paul was beheaded, the giant facade now has mosaics depicting Paul with a sword and Peter with the keys. But Peter was never in Rome.

Another church in Rome is called Church of St. Peter in Chains.

And, of course, the tradition is that Peter was crucified at Rome and feeling not fit to be crucified like Jesus he asked to be crucified head downward. That is pure manufactured tradition.

Paul died at Rome and was beheaded. There is no reason to believe that back at Rome at that time they were crucifying prisoners, and there is not any inference in history or any reliable information anywhere that Peter was ever at Rome or that he died there.

IV. PETER WAS NEVER AT ROME, WAS NEVER A POPE

The very basis for the giant monstrosity that is the Roman Catholic Church is that Peter was at Rome, that he was the first pope, that other popes and the Catholic priesthood are all fulfilling the position and charge and work given to Peter.

And all that is utterly false, since Peter was never at Rome. And Peter was never a pope, could not have been.

1. Peter Was Not at Rome When Paul Wrote the Book of Romans

In Romans 16 Paul greets twenty-nine people, besides sending greetings to the church that gathers in one person's house, the brethren of others "and all the saints which are with them." Naming twenty-nine people, Paul does not mention Peter. He mentions casual acquaintances, old friends and those he had met elsewhere. But he does not mention Peter. Peter was not in Rome. It would be unthinkable for one apostle to write to that far-off capital city and write lovingly of twenty-nine different people and not mention the other apostle, if he were there. He was not there.

2. Peter Was Not in Rome When Paul Arrived in Acts 28

When Paul arrived at Rome, "Paul was suffered to dwell by himself with a soldier that kept him. And it came to pass, that after three days Paul called the chief of the Jews together" and talked to them (Acts 28:16,17). And these Jews in Rome had heard nothing about Paul nor even about the Christian religion. They said, "But we desire to hear of thee what thou thinkest: for as concerning this sect, we know that every where it is spoken against" (vs. 22). So they appointed a day and Paul spoke to them about Jesus. Some were saved and some were not. And Paul lived two years in his own hired house and Peter is not even mentioned. He was not there. It is unthinkable that Paul could be in Rome, could meet all the other principal Jews and Peter not even be mentioned, if he were there.

3. Paul Wrote From Rome Again and Again and Never Mentioned Peter

The Letter to the Ephesians was written from Rome in A.D. 64 to the Christians at Ephesus. Tychicus carried the letter, but no mention is made of Peter.

The Letter to the Philippians was written from Rome, and it was addressed from "Paul and Timotheus, the servants of Jesus Christ, to all the saints in Christ Jesus which are at Philippi, with the bishops and deacons." Not from Peter; Peter wasn't there.

The Epistle to the Colossians was written by "Paul, an apostle of Jesus Christ by the will of God, and Timotheus our brother." Not from Peter. And to these Colossian Christians he mentioned

Onesimus, Aristarchus, Marcus or Mark (sister's son to Barnabas), Jesus which is called Justus, Epaphras, Luke the beloved physician and Demas. These all sent greetings. No greetings from Peter; Peter was not at Rome.

The Epistle to Philemon was written from Rome, from "Paul, a prisoner of Jesus Christ, and Timothy our brother, unto Philemon. . . ." And he sent salutations from Epaphras, Marcus, Aristarchus, Demas and Lucas; none from Peter.

Second Timothy was written from this imprisonment at Rome, also, very soon before Paul was beheaded. And Paul wrote, "For Demas hath forsaken me, having loved this present world, and is departed unto Thessalonica; Crescens to Galatia, Titus unto Dalmatia. Only Luke is with me. Take Mark, and bring him with thee: for he is profitable to me for the ministry. And Tychicus have I sent to Ephesus."

Who is with Paul? "Only Luke is with me." And he sent greetings from Eubulus, and Pudens, and Linus, and Claudia, and all the brethren. No greeting from Peter. Peter wasn't at Rome. Only Luke was with him of the Christian workers.

4. Peter Was Not at Rome Because He Was Committed to Preach the Gospel to the Jews, to the Circumcised

Paul went up to Jerusalem and talked to the apostles, he tells us in Galatians 1 and 2. And in Galatians 2:7-9 we read their decision:

"But contrariwise, when they saw that the gospel of the uncircumcision was committed unto me, as the gospel of the circumcision was unto Peter; (For he that wrought effectually in Peter to the apostleship of the circumcision, the same was mighty in me toward the Gentiles:) And when James, Cephas, and John, who seemed to be pillars, perceived the grace that was given unto me, they gave to me and Barnabas the right hands of fellowship; that we should go unto the heathen, and they unto the circumcision."

"The gospel of the uncircumcision," that is, to Gentiles, was committed to Paul, verse 7 says, as "the gospel of the circumcision," that is, to the Jews, was unto Peter. James and Cephas (that is Peter) and John saw that God's grace was with Paul.

They gave him and Barnabas the right hand of fellowship that
Paul and Barnabas should go to the heathen (Gentiles) while
they (James, Peter and John) should go to the circumcision. It
was clearly the leading of God that Paul should go to the Gentiles
and Peter should not.

5. Peter Went to the Jews of the Dispersion in Old Babylon

Peter left Jerusalem and went to Babylon to preach to the
Jews left there. Just as God put it into the heart of Paul to preach
to the Gentiles, He put it on the heart of Peter to preach particularly to Jews. Actually, Peter was not led of God and was not
fitted in mind to preach to the Gentiles. It took a miraculous
message from God to get Peter even to go to Cornelius to preach.
And Peter was so anxious not to displease the Jews from
Jerusalem that we read in Galatians 2:11-14:

*"But when Peter was come to Antioch, I withstood him to the
face, because he was to be blamed. For before that certain came
from James, he did eat with the Gentiles: but when they were
come, he withdrew and separated himself, fearing them which
were of the circumcision. And the other Jews dissembled likewise
with him; insomuch that Barnabas also was carried away with
their dissimulation. But when I saw that they walked not up-
rightly according to the truth of the gospel, I said unto Peter
before them all, If thou, being a Jew, livest after the manner of
Gentiles, and not as do the Jews, why compellest thou the Gentiles to live as do the Jews?"*

Peter was not called to preach to Gentiles, did not have the
heart attitude from God for it. He went to the Jews in Babylon.

The First Epistle of Peter is addressed "to the strangers [so-
journers of the dispersion] scattered throughout Pontus,
Galatia, Cappadocia, Asia, and Bithynia." Not to Gentiles but
to Jews. This letter, of course, was inspired and so is good for
everybody. It was written from Babylon and in I Peter 5:13 it
says, "The church that is at Babylon, elected together with you,
saluteth you; and so doth Marcus my son." And II Peter also,
doubtless, was written from Babylon, and in the old King James

Version of the Bible the book was regularly introduced as from Babylon.

Peter was not at Rome. That is a human tradition not founded on the Bible, manufactured for the purpose of claiming power over the souls of men.

V. TRADITION BUILT THE IDOLATROUS CULT OF MARY

Consider the cult of Mary in the official Catholic doctrine. Catholic leaders deny that this is idolatry, but in simple truth most Catholics love Mary better than they love Jesus. Mary is called "Mother of God." She is called "Queen of Heaven." Catholic teachers often call her "the Mediatrix," that is, the mediator between God and man. Thus she is actually given credit that ought to go to Christ the Son of God Himself, and that, of course, is idolatry.

It is now official doctrine that Mary had an immaculate conception, not referring to the virgin birth of Christ but referring to her own conception. And so it is taught that Mary is without the taint of Adamic sin and never sinned. It is taught, as Catholic official doctrine, that Mary ascended bodily to Heaven. Thus Catholics are taught that, like Jesus, Mary was sinless; like the Lord Jesus, she arose from the dead; like the Lord Jesus, she is a mediator between God and man, to whom we should pray. And all this goes against the clear teaching of the Word of God.

1. Mary was specially favored in one particular matter—that is, in that she was allowed to conceive and bear in her body the body of the Lord Jesus. She is not the "Mother of God," but mother of the human body of Jesus. So the angel said to Mary, "Hail, thou that art highly favoured, the Lord is with thee: blessed art thou among women" (Luke 1:28). It is never said that she was especially blessed in any other matter more than other women.

2. Mary plainly confessed her sinful state when she said, "And my spirit hath rejoiced in God my Saviour" (Luke 1:47). The only one who needs a Saviour is a sinner. Mary is confessing her sinfulness, her part along with the rest of the fallen race, as needing a Saviour and taking Jesus as Saviour.

3. Jesus plainly said that, instead of Mary's being especially blessed because she bore the Saviour and nursed Him as a Baby, rather anyone who hears and keeps the Word of God is as blessed as Mary. Luke 11:27,28 says:

"And it came to pass, as he spake these things, a certain woman of the company lifted up her voice, and said unto him, Blessed is the womb that bare thee, and the paps which thou hast sucked. But he said, Yea rather, blessed are they that hear the word of God, and keep it."

Once when Jesus was teaching and preaching, His mother and His brothers came inquiring for Him. Luke 8:19-21 tells us:

"Then came to him his mother and his brethren, and could not come at him for the press. And it was told him by certain which said, Thy mother and thy brethren stand without, desiring to see thee. And he answered and said unto them, My mother and my brethren are these which hear the word of God, and do it."

Notice that not the mother of Jesus nor those who were His mother's sons, but all "which hear the word of God, and do it" are as good as Christ's mother and His brethren. And this is so important that God has it written down also in Matthew 12:46-50, in Mark 3:31-35.

Any good woman, saved by trusting Christ and then hearing the Word of God and doing it, believing on Christ, is as great and as blessed as Mary, in the relationship to God.

4. It is quite clear that in New Testament times nobody gave Mary any prominence over other Christian women. After the resurrection of Christ, she is mentioned only once and that is in Acts 1:14. She attended a prayer meeting! She is never mentioned in the rest of the book of Acts, not in any of the New Testament epistles. Thus tradition has made the Word of God of none effect.

VI. THE APOSTLE PAUL AT ROME

Paul was at Rome for some years. Peter was never there. It is shocking that most of the Catholic tradition in Rome is about Peter, not about Paul. The giant Basilica of St. Peters is named for Peter, and it is falsely claimed that his bones are buried there. There is the Church of St. Peter in Chains which contains the famous statue of Moses by Michelangelo.

In the Mamertine Prison, it is openly taught that Peter was imprisioned there and the plaque is principally about Peter, not Paul, though Peter was never there. In the Church of St. Paul-Outside-the-Walls, Peter is emphasized as well as Paul. Pictured on the wall are all the popes, beginning with Peter. But the simple fact is, Paul was the great Christian who went to Rome and took the Gospel there. Peter was never at Rome.

1. Paul Was Evidently Imprisoned at Rome Twice

He was in his own hired house two years, and given great freedom in his first imprisonment (Acts 28:16). But he must have been released for a season and then re-arrested and eventually beheaded there. The evidence of a second imprisonment is strong.

First, in Philemon, verse 22, Paul wrote from Rome, "But withal prepare me also a lodging: for I trust that through your prayers I shall be given unto you." He would be released.

Second, in Philippians 1:25,26 Paul said, "And having this confidence, I know that I shall abide and continue with you all for your furtherance and joy of faith; That your rejoicing may be more abundant in Jesus Christ for me by my coming to you again." Notice Paul said, "I know. . . ." He is coming to Philippi again.

Third, in II Timothy 4:20 Paul said, ". . .but Trophimus have I left at Miletum sick." But in his journey to Rome the first time, as we see in Acts 27, Trophimus is not mentioned as being present and they did not stop at Miletum. So Paul must be referring to a second trip to Rome and to his second imprisonment.

Fourth, Paul had it revealed to him that he should go to Spain. In Romans 15:24 he said, "Whensoever I take my journey into Spain, I will come to you: for I trust to see you in my journey, and to be brought on my way thitherward by you, if first I be somewhat filled with your company." Again he was inspired to say, ". . .I will come by you into Spain" (Rom. 15:28). So Paul did not have it revealed to him that he would go to Rome as a prisoner, but it was revealed to him to go to Rome and that he would go on to Spain. Then he must have been released from his first imprisonment, went to Spain, returned to Philippi, stayed with Philemon as he had promised, eventually going back to Rome, then was arrested and finally martyred there.

Mamertine prison is under this church

2. His Farewell From the Dungeon
We believe that the Mamertine dungeon was probably the

death house from which Paul wrote his last letters and from where he went to his death. In II Timothy 4:6-13 Paul wrote:

"For I am now ready to be offered, and the time of my departure is at hand. I have fought a good fight, I have finished my course, I have kept the faith: Henceforth there is laid up for me a crown of righteousness, which the Lord, the righteous judge, shall give me at that day: and not to me only, but unto all them also that love his appearing. Do thy diligence to come shortly unto me: For Demas hath forsaken me, having loved this present world, and is departed unto Thessalonica; Crescens to Galatia, Titus unto Dalmatia. Only Luke is with me. Take Mark, and bring him with thee: for he is profitable to me for the ministry. And Tychicus have I sent to Ephesus. The cloke that I left at Troas with Carpus, when thou comest, bring with thee, and the books, but especially the parchments."

Then in verse 21 he said, "Do thy diligence to come before winter." Paul is alone in the prison, with no one but Luke with him. Demas found the road too hard and, having loved the present world, he forsook Paul. Crescens has gone to Galatia, Titus to Dalmatia, and we are not told whether they left embarrassed by Paul's imprisonment or whether they went to serve under God's leading. But Paul was alone.

That underground stone prison, about seventeen feet across, the ceiling only about seven feet and at that time with only a round hole through which the prisoner could enter or be taken out and through which food could be provided, may have been cold in winter. So Paul wrote to Timothy, "Please bring the cloke that I left at Troas." He was thinking that if he did not die before winter, he would need it then. It was cold in that old underground dungeon.

And some books—if Timothy could bring the books, especially "the parchments," it would make the hours as he waited the headsman's ax that much shorter and sweeter.

3. God Let Paul Know His Death Approached
Paul said, "I am now ready to be offered, and the time of my

departure is at hand." God, in His loving mercy, had let Paul know he would soon die as a martyr, a sacrifice, and Paul was ready. Evidently the Apostle Peter, likewise, was warned ahead of time that death was approaching, for in II Peter 1:14 he said, "Knowing that shortly I must put off this my tabernacle, even as our Lord Jesus Christ hath shewed me."

I think that Simeon, the ancient, godly man waiting for the birth of Jesus, knew that, now that he had seen the Saviour, he would die and go on to Heaven (Luke 2:19).

My dear father had a conviction that he would know when the time of his death approached, and he did. Once he was desperately sick and not expected to live. I was called back from a revival campaign in Vinton, Louisiana, to rush to his deathbed. But when I arrived, he was sitting propped in an overstuffed chair because he could not breathe lying down and he said to me, "No, Son, I am not going yet. I will know when the time comes."

He lived for two years more. He had had a stroke. He walked with difficulty, but as he got more and more control of his movements, one day he slipped away and drove his car two hundred miles up to Duke, Oklahoma, where I was in a revival campaign. But meantime he went by to see my cousin Georgia and said to her, "Well, Georgia, I wanted to come by and see you before I go to be with the Lord."

She said to him, "Why, Uncle Willie, you look stronger than usual. You have been gaining strength."

"Yes," he said, "but my life is finished; my children are grown, my wife is gone, and now God is ready for me to come Home."

Before he left home that day he had talked with some men who were building a store building for him and he said, "Now are the instructions very clear and the contract clear, the kind of material, the roof, etc.?" The contractor told him, "Yes." And my father said, "Well, remember now, because I won't be here when it is finished and I want it done right."

So he came to Duke, Oklahoma, to the revival. There he won four men, heads of families, to Christ. Then he came in one evening at 5:00 with heart trouble. We called the doctor, and in an hour he went Home to be with the Lord. He knew the time was at hand.

Well, so did Paul. And isn't it sweet when one has a hungry heart for Heaven and now he knows the time he has longed for is here? He had written the Christians at Philippi that "to die is gain" and "I am in a strait betwixt two, having a desire to depart, and to be with Christ; which is far better: Nevertheless to abide in the flesh is more needful for you" (Phil. 1:21,23,24). So now Paul said, "I am now ready to be offered."

Oh, Paul, you have been ready a long time, haven't you? Remember, he had written, "I die daily." I think he meant what Jesus commanded us to mean, that is, he took up his cross daily to follow Jesus and faced death. Everywhere he went he got beatings, shipwreck, abuse, hunger, thirst and jail. Now the happy time has come when he will see the Lord! Paul had labored hard, because he said, ". . .that. . .we may be accepted of him" (II Cor. 5:9). He has no fear now facing the Lord Jesus he had loved so well.

He said, "I have fought a good fight, I have finished my course, I have kept the faith." Ah, Paul, you did fight a good fight. You fought the beasts at Ephesus (I Cor. 15:32), and faced the mob of idolaters. You faced Peter when he compromised and would not eat with Gentile converts (Gal. 2:11,12). You faced Elymas the sorcerer with boldness in the power of God and he was stricken blind, and Sergius Paulus was converted. You were not ashamed to stand before Felix and Festus and Agrippa and Herod to give your testimony and preach Christ! Now there awaits a mighty crown for you and you can rejoice as you go to meet the Saviour.

A group of us pilgrims stood in that Mamertine dungeon, and I read Paul's farewell message. They looked at the bare walls and felt the chill there, and they could see what it cost to be the kind of Christian Paul was. Then we sang together,

> **Faith of our fathers! living still**
> **In spite of dungeon, fire, and sword:**
> **O how our hearts beat high with joy**
> **Whene'er we hear that glorious word!**
> **Faith of our fathers! holy faith!**
> **We will be true to thee till death!**

A service in Mamertine

Our fathers, chained in prisons dark,
  Were still in heart and conscience free:
How sweet would be their children's fate,
  If they, like them, could die for thee!
Faith of our fathers! holy faith!
  We will be true to thee till death!

Faith of our fathers! we will love
  Both friend and foe in all our strife:
And preach thee, too, as love knows how,
  By kindly words and virtuous life:
Faith of our fathers! holy faith!
  We will be true to thee till death!

Then I called on a dear old Tennessee pastor to pray. And with tears he prayed, "Lord, don't let any of us ever complain about anything any more!"

Yes, Paul was at Rome. And he was sure when he came that he had come "in the fulness of the blessing of the gospel of Christ" and so he did (Rom. 15:29). And what a heritage he left to the world of a Christian wholly dedicated and willing to die to win souls; and die he did.

II. Paul on Mars' Hill and
"the Bema" at Corinth

Fourteen times, as I led groups to visit the important places in the Holy Land, we stopped in Greece. There are two spots that draw Christian tourists like a magnet. One of them is Mars' Hill, that little eminence half way up the slopes of the Acropolis, a solid mound of stone where Paul came and preached his wonderful sermon recorded in the 17th chapter of Acts.

The other place is the ruins of ancient Corinth where Paul preached for eighteen months and left a thriving church and to whom he wrote the First and Second Corinthian epistles. I love to go to those two places and rehearse the ministry of Paul there.

You remember the Apostle Paul was "the apostle of the Gentiles." That was his calling. He wanted to go back to preach to his beloved Jews in Jerusalem but was forbidden to do so. And when he did go later, he was arrested. God had said, "I will send thee far hence unto the Gentiles."

Peter, after preaching at Jerusalem, had gone to Babylon to the dispersed Jews left there after the captivity and many others who had joined them. Other apostles had preached in many places to the Jews. Probably Thomas had gone to the Jews in India; there were many Jews there then, as now.

Paul must go then toward the center of Gentile culture and government in the world. He must go to Greece and to Rome. Greece had taken the world empire away from the Media-Persians under the swift and mighty genius of Alexander the Great. Then after Alexander died and the kingdom divided to his four generals, Rome became the center of world empire and government.

I. PAUL COMES FROM ASIA TO GREECE

Greece, while losing political government over the world, yet did not give up cultural leadership. They had conquered the world with their art, their philosophies, their literature. Rome, militarily victorious, took Greeks as teachers. Greek plays were acted out in Roman theaters and stadia all over the civilized world. Greek architects were employed in great Roman buildings. The Greek language became the second language everywhere, more than Latin of Rome. So the barriers between the states crumbled and nations were united under the Roman control.

Galatians 4:4 says, *"But when the fulness of the time was come, God sent forth his Son, made of a woman, made under the law."* It was the fullness of time when the prophecies were fulfilled and it was time for Christ to be born, according to Old Testament Scriptures. But it was the fullness of time also in that now the world had become largely one nation and one did not have to fight to cross boundaries. Now Paul would be able to go from Judaea into Cilicia, Galatia, Asia, and then over into Europe to Macedonia (Northern Greece) and Achaia (Southern Greece). And all the time Paul could preach in the Koine Greek language in which all his epistles would be written. God got the world ready for Christ and the Gospel, and Paul now must take the Gospel to the great centers of the Gentiles.

1. Into Europe at Philippi

Paul had earnestly waited on the Lord. The Holy Spirit would not allow him to go into the neighboring provinces. But in the night a vision appeared, and a man of Macedonia besought him, "Come over into Macedonia, and help us." So, with companions, Paul sailed from Troas and came to Neapolis in upper Greece, Macedonia, and then to Philippi.

We suppose he did not stop to preach before he got to Philippi. There he stayed for some time. Jewish women met for a prayer meeting out by the riverside and Paul met with them. A good number were converted, as we read in Acts 16.

Ah, but a poor slave girl, devil-possessed, told fortunes and

The Acropolis as seen from Mars' Hill

made her masters much money. Paul was grieved at the sight. At last he got the courage and faith to command the devils to come out of the girl, and they did, and she told fortunes no more.

How angry were her masters! They accused Paul and Silas, their clothes were torn off, they were beaten and fastened in the stocks in the jail. Ah, but at midnight Paul and Silas prayed and sang praises to God and the prisoners heard them. Yes, and up in Heaven they heard, too! Soon there was a shivering tremble, a rumble, and the old jail began to rock, the door burst open and the bars from the windows, the stocks cracked open enabling them to relieve their strained ankles from the wooden notches, and Paul and Silas were free.

The jailor waked out of sleep and would have killed himself, supposing the prisoners were fled, but Paul said, "Do thyself no harm: for we are all here." Then there follows the earnest plea of the jailor, the question asked, "What must I do to be saved?" and answered so plainly, "Believe on the Lord Jesus Christ, and thou shalt be saved, and thy house." Oh, and all that family were saved that night.

Aren't we glad for such a clear statement of the Gospel? We may tell sinners anywhere, "Believe on the Lord Jesus Christ, and thou shalt be saved."

But Paul is a Roman citizen. When the rulers of the city hear that, they urge him to slip away, but Paul said, "No, sir!" They must come and bring him out publicly. And they did.

Philippi was always dear to Paul. You can sense it in the loving praises he uses in his letter to the Philippians later.

Slippery steps to Mars' Hill

2. Thessalonica and Jews Who Cause Riot

Then Paul went to Thessalonica. It is still a good sized city, in Northern Greece, and there he preached the Gospel in the synagogue of the Jews. You see, Jews were scattered over the world, and so, Paul found a synagogue here. First, many would hear about it, then some Jews, perhaps who had heard about this Christian religion from Jerusalem, hated Paul and opposed him and brought riots there. Paul preached and won some souls and left.

But he left Christians here and his two letters to the Thessalonians show that good, solid works were left where Paul had preached the Gospel.

3. To Berea, "More Noble Than Those in Thessalonica"

On to Berea Paul went and preached in the synagogue there, and "these were more noble than those in Thessalonica, in that they received the word with all readiness of mind, and searched the scriptures daily, whether those things were so" (Acts 17:11).

Noble Bereans! A wonderful thing is said of them—they studied the Scriptures to see if these things were so.

Paul did not stay long there. The Jews who hated Paul and the Gospel came from Thessalonica to stir up trouble here. Paul slipped away as if he were going to the sea coast, but they took him on down to Athens, in the province of Achaia (Southern Greece). And there he sent word for Timothy and Silas to come to him there.

Now Paul is in Athens.

4. Paul's Burning Heart in Athens

Paul was now in the center of the culture of the world. That beautiful temple to Athena, the Parthenon, some say the most beautiful building ever built, stood out on the Acropolis to mark Athens as the center of idolatry in the world. Oh, they worshiped many, many gods, and there were many idols and shrines to prove it.

Athens was a city of wealth, and a large majority owned slaves and needed to do no work. It was a country of philosophers, artists and writers. They liked the writings of Homer; they acted out the plays of famous Greek authors; they inspected the sculpture of the greatest artists. Pericles, Plato and Aristotle had formed schools of philosophy and teaching. So there was an intellectualism in Athens, along with flagrant idolatry.

How the heart of Paul burned as he saw the city wholly given to idolatry; so he began to preach Jesus. While people were not greatly interested in his religion, they were interested in the philosophy he taught. They said, "This babbler. . .seemeth to be a setter forth of strange gods." So they took him to Mars'

Hill where was the center of discussion, the center of idolatry and philosophy in Athens.

II. PAUL ON MARS' HILL

Mars' Hill is a mound of stone and with slippery steps now that you must climb carefully. Then, no doubt, the steps were not so worn. Even now there are squared-out places where once sat idols and shrines. That little hill is bald now except for these marks of an ancient culture and idolatry. But they brought Paul there to speak.

The author and Mrs. Rice on Mars' Hill

1. Paul Had a Holy Compassion for These Given Over to Idolatry

I remember the first time I stopped at the Church of the Holy Stairs in Rome. There Catholic tradition says Queen Helena, mother of Emperor Constantine, brought twenty-eight steps from the Fortress of Antonia where was Pilate's judgment hall in Jerusalem and they said these steps are the very steps on which Christ walked that day. So a church was built around these twenty-eight steps. I saw people climbing on their knees. Many of them stop to pray on every step and kiss the one ahead. Many are in tears. About fourteen times I have seen this same scene. My heart breaks within me as I see how they seek with tears, and perhaps with penitence, to find God. Oh, there is a better way to God than climbing on bruised knees up some so-called holy steps! But I know how Paul felt when he looked on those people worshiping idols.

I wonder, reader, if we do not need—oh, surely we need more of this holy compassion which Paul had!

Dr. J. L. Ward was president of Decatur College, Decatur, Texas, when I attended there. He had been a roommate of Dr. George W. Truett in Baylor University, and often went to visit with Dr. Truett in Dallas.

He told me how one time he had gone to visit with Dr. Truett and from the First Baptist Church they went out to lunch. As they crossed Akard Street, with its sidewalks filled with people at noon rushing here and yonder, and cars in the streets everywhere, they stopped at a corner. Dr. Truett stood, he said, oblivious to the changing of traffic lights, and gazed. At last he turned with quivering lips and said to Dr. Ward, "Ward, they are lost! They are lost! Look at that crowd! They are lost!"

So Paul looked upon the people at Athens and went gladly to Mars' Hill to tell them about Jesus.

2. Paul Openly Attacks Their Idolatry

Did they think that a god made with men's hands was any god at all? And Paul told them boldly that he came to tell them of a God whom they in ignorance had put up a sign about, "To the unknown God." He told them that the God who made all this universe was not a God to be made with men's hands.

He did not preach one god among many others, but the only God. He did not suggest a culture of mingled Greek philosophy and revelation; he preached to them the Creator, One who

". . .giveth to all life, and breath, and all things; And hath made of one blood all nations of men for to dwell on all the face of the earth, and hath determined the times before appointed, and the bounds of their habitation; That they should seek the Lord, if *haply they might feel after him, and find him, though he be not far from every one of us."*

He said that all of us are the offspring, in the sense of being the creatures that God made. He is saying that idols are utterly worthless, and any religion but the religion of God who made us and of Christ His Son who died for us is foolish and useless.

3. He Solemnly Warned Them of Judgment

What great preaching Paul did here! He declared:

"And the times of this ignorance God winked at; but now commandeth all men every where to repent: Because he hath appointed a day, in the which he will judge the world in righteousness by that man whom he hath ordained; whereof he hath given assurance unto all men, in that he hath raised him from the dead."—Acts 17:30,31.

It is a religion of Christ that he preaches. They are coming to judgment for their sins. Always we ought to start with sinners on the matter of sin. It is to be clearly stated or implied or understood—men are lost sinners who need to be born again. "The wages of sin is death," and sin leads to Hell, and so God has warned men that they must repent. God was merciful to people in ignorance, but now has commanded all men everywhere to repent. And He has appointed a day in which Christ Himself will judge the world. God has personally put His eternal approval on Christ in raising Him from the dead.

There was not much obvious and immediate results here. Paul left them but, "Howbeit certain men clave unto him, and believed: among the which was Dionysius the Areopagite, and a woman named Damaris, and others with them" (Acts 17:34).

I love to stand on that mound of rock and look among what I can imagine of the people that day as Paul faced them and told them boldly there is no hope but in Jesus Christ!

III. PAUL AT CORINTH

Again and again it has been our privilege to take the fine road sixty miles west from Athens out on to the Peloponnesian peninsula and there on the Isthmus that joins this great Pelopennesian

The BEMA, judgment place in Corinth

Ancient road led from the Bema to the sea coast

peninsula to the main body of Greece. A little peninsula, only four miles wide, connects this body over a hundred miles north and south and a hundred miles east and west, to the main body. And now a great canal across this Isthmus joins the gulf of Corinth on the north, and connects with the Ionian Sea and the Aegean Sea and the Mediterranean on the south.

It is a beautiful drive, with the Bay of Salamis on our left where the Greeks in a great Naval battle centuries before Paul defeated the much greater fleet of the Persians; with mountains and olive vineyards on the right. It was thrilling to stand on the bridge across the canal and see ships coming through that four-mile cut that saves them two hundred miles when they come from Adriatic ports down to Athens or back.

As we go along in the big buses we wonder, Did the Apostle Paul walk along the seaside here going from Athens to Corinth? Or did he perhaps sail in a ship from near Athens up to Cenchrea on the peninsula, and then walk to Corinth? Or did he ride a donkey? At any rate, it so interests us to know that Paul came along this way to Corinth. Because Paul preached in Corinth for a year and a half and because he wrote I Corinthinas and II Corinthians as his letters to the great church there, we are so glad to visit the excavated ruins of Corinth.

1. Paul Tells Us How He Felt as He Came This Way From Athens to Corinth

In I Corinthians 2:1-4 he says:

"And I, brethren, when I came to you, came not with excellency of speech or of wisdom, declaring unto you the testimony of God. For I determined not to know any thing among you, save Jesus Christ, and him crucified. And I was with you in weakness, and in fear, and in much trembling. And my speech and my preaching was not with enticing words of man's wisdom, but in demonstration of the Spirit and of power."

Paul was "in weakness, and in fear, and in much trembling." Why?

Well, he was going to the greatest city he had ever entered. There were more than a quarter of a million people here. It was much larger than Jerusalem or Caesarea or Antioch or Lystra or Derbe or Troas; larger than Philippi, Thessalonica, Berea; larger even than Athens. Paul felt compelled to bring the Gospel to the great Gentile centers of the world. But I understand how he felt when he came.

Again and again in great citywide revival campaigns I have sometimes faced a giant tent full of people or a public auditorium like the Arena in Chicago, Kleinhans Music Hall in Buffalo, the Public Music Hall in Cleveland, Liberty Tobacco Warehouse in Winston-Salem, the Municipal Auditorium in Miami, and I have gone with great anticipation, but I must confess with fear and trembling, for that first service. Oh, how I prayed, "Lord, give me their hearts tonight! Lord, get hold of them tonight with power so they will come back and so we can have conviction and souls saved."

And not only was Corinth a great city, but it was the most immoral of all the great cities in the world. There by the city was the mountain, the Acro-Corinthus, that is, the Acropolis, a mountain which was their watchtower and place of refuge, and their place of worship. Serving the idol temple there in their religion was a thousand prostitutes. Immorality was so widespread as to be famous. Even Christians there would be continually tempted to go into the sin so prevalent and so accepted. It is not surprising that Paul later needed to rebuke these Corinthian Christians, for a man was living in adultery with his mother-in-law and the church did not mind. People got drunk at the Lord's Table. They fussed over eating meats offered to idols. They had a great heresy of tongues. And so ahead of time Paul would tremble at the thought of going to this great city.

Remember, too, that Paul is a Jew and that his main contact has been with Jews. It is true he preached in Philippi, Thessalonica, Berea and in Athens, but in two of those places he got run out by a mob (in Thessalonica and Berea), and in Athens he was not very successful. And here he feels that though he is called as an apostle to the Gentiles, how can he know the reaction that will meet him? So he came "in fear, and in much trembling."

It may be, too, that the lack of much success in Athens has humbled him.

There had been no special persecutions in Athens.

"And when they heard of the resurrection of the dead, some mocked: and others said, We will hear thee again of this matter. So Paul departed from among them. Howbeit certain men clave unto him, and believed: among the which was Dionysius the Areopagite, and a woman named Damaris, and others with them."—Acts 17:32-34.

Paul went shame-faced from Athens, we suppose. Some way he felt he had failed; he had not had the great results he had hoped to have and had had elsewhere.

He quoted the poets and the philosophers in his address to Athens on Mars' Hill. Is that why he said to the Corinthians,

"For I determined not to know any thing among you, save Jesus Christ, and him crucified," and why he said, *"And my speech and my preaching was not with enticing words of man's wisdom, but in demonstration of the Spirit and of power."*—I Cor. 2:2,4?

Ah, Paul, God is going to bless you greatly in Corinth!

2. Paul Makes Tents for a Living

In Corinth Paul

". . .found a certain Jew named Aquila, born in Pontus, lately come from Italy, with his wife Priscilla; (because that Claudius had commanded all Jews to depart from Rome:) and came unto them. And because he was of the same craft, he abode with them, and wrought: for by their occupation they were tentmakers."—Acts 18:2,3.

It was tradition among rabbis and learned Jews that every man ought to have a trade and even the rabbis who spent much of their time in teaching the law felt obligated to have some way to earn a living otherwise. So Paul was a tentmaker and worked with Aquila and Priscilla and lived with them.

I would judge they are already Christians. Paul found them a great help to him.

And they were such good Christians that later when Paul left

Corinth he took with him Priscilla and Aquila and left them at Ephesus (Acts 18:18,19). And there in Ephesus they were able to take the fine preacher Apollos to one side and show him the Word of God more perfectly, since he had not had any of the teaching the apostles had received personally from Jesus and had not been present at Pentecost. These are godly, good people.

Later we find they must have returned to Rome for in his letter to the Romans, written, the scholars say, on his third visit to Corinth and so after this time, he sent greetings to Aquila and Priscilla and to "the church that is in their house" (Rom. 16:3,5). What a comfort to a man of God to find somebody with a loving heart to provide and work with them!

Paul was not above hard labor. Though he knows that "they which preach the gospel should live of the gospel" by God's plan, and though he plainly commands Timothy, "Let the elders that rule well be counted worthy of double honour, especially they who labour in the word and doctrine. For the scripture saith, Thou shalt not muzzle the ox that treadeth out the corn. And, The labourer is worthy of his reward" (I Tim. 5:17,18), yet he did not require support for himself. So he worked the long week days and on the Sabbath days he entered the synagogue and preached the Gospel.

And he will write also to those of Thessalonica, reminding them that when he was among them he wrote, "Neither did we eat any man's bread for nought; but wrought with labour and travail night and day, that we might not be chargeable to any of you" (II Thess. 3:8).

But Paul did have some godly help now in Corinth for he wrote to his friends at Philippi, "Now ye Philippians know also, that in the beginning of the gospel, when I departed from Macedonia, no church communicated with me as concerning giving and receiving, but ye only" (Phil. 4:15). They had even supported him in Thessalonica.

At Athens Paul had sent word to Timothy and Titus to come quickly to meet him. Now at Corinth, in Acts 18:5 it is said, "And when Silas and Timotheus were come from Macedonia, Paul was pressed in the spirit, and testified to the Jews that

Jesus was Christ." Now how vigorously he preached and we suppose, every day, and it is likely that Timothy and Titus brought gifts from the Philippians so Paul could go on preaching every day!

What a lesson for all of us! God never intended that preachers should live a life of ease. It is not necessary that a preacher have all the luxuries or even the comforts that other people sometimes have. Paul did not have them. As the Lord Jesus must sometimes sleep on the ground, because the foxes had holes and the birds of the air had nests, but He had not where to lay His head, even so Paul himself was in fastings often, in nakedness and in distress.

God bless every man who, like Paul, sets out to pay any price to preach the Gospel, whether he gets paid or not, and to preach the Gospel even if he has to work every day. But I am glad others made it possible part of the time for Paul to preach every day.

3. God's Abundant Blessing on Paul at Corinth

I can understand Paul's fear and trembling as he came to face that giant city of iniquity and idolatry, Corinth. And he had gotten run out of Thessalonica and Berea. He had been stoned and left for dead at Lystra. He had been beaten and put in jail at Philippi. It is not surprising that Paul tried to hold himself ready to die at any time and said, "I die daily" (I Cor. 15:31).

But at Corinth God gave him great success. Jews in the synagogue blasphemed and opposed themselves and so he said to them, "Your blood be upon your own heads; I am clean: from henceforth I will go unto the Gentiles" (Acts 18:6). So he moved into a house next door, the home of Justus, a godly man, and Crispus, the chief ruler of the synagogue, was saved. Then many, many other Corinthians were saved and baptized.

One night the Lord came to Saul in a vision and said, "Be not afraid, but speak, and hold not thy peace: For I am with thee, and no man shall set on thee to hurt thee: for I have much people in this city" (Acts 18:9,10). Oh, what comfort it is to preach, knowing that God is with you!

Of course, the Jews made an insurrection against Paul. They seized him and brought him to the Bema, the judgment seat. I have been there many times in the ruins of Old Corinth, the place that was known as the judgment seat. I stood, very likely, about where Paul stood.

But Gallio was the deputy, that is, the Roman governor of the province of Achaia, including Athens, of which Corinth was the capital. And Gallio was kindly toward Paul. He was a brother of the philosopher Seneca, we are told. And when the Jews argued against Paul, Gallio drove them from the judgment seat and said, "I will be no judge of such matters!"

I walked up and down that pavement now exposed by excavation. I saw the long row of business houses on each side of that principal street. I imagined the dear apostle going from day to day for eighteen months preaching the Gospel. Oh, how many were saved! And a great congregation was established there to whom Paul would write his letters of I Corinthians and II Corinthians!

There are lessons for us here. In the first place, why do not we make great plans for God? Paul picked out the largest cities, the cities where he must start from scratch, with no help, to get out the Gospel. He understood the thought of Psalm 81:10 where God said, "I am the Lord thy God, which brought thee out of the land of Egypt: open thy mouth wide, and I will fill it." Paul expected great things. He might tremble, but he went on in faith just the same, and God blessed him.

We should learn also that as the Apostle Paul did not put money first and made no demands for himself, worked to earn his own bread when necessary, so we ought to start out by all means to get out the Gospel, paid or unpaid, recognized or not recognized. Paul did not have to have the luxuries of the time, nor do we.

SO SEND I YOU

So send I you to labor unrewarded,
To serve unpaid, unloved, unsought, unknown,
To bear rebuke, to suffer scorn and scoffing—
So send I you to toil for Me alone.

So send I you to bind the bruised and broken,
O'er wand'ring souls to work, to weep, to wake,
To bear the burdens of a world aweary—

Ruins of ancient Corinth

So send I you to suffer for My sake.

So send I you to loneliness and longing,
With heart a-hung'ring for the loved and known,
Forsaking home and kindred, friend and dear one—
So send I you to know My love alone.

So send I you to leave your life's ambition,
To die to dear desire, self-will resign,
To labor long, and love where men revile you—
So send I you to lose your life in Mine.

So send I you to hearts made hard by hatred,
To eyes made blind because they will not see,
To spend, tho' it be blood, to spend and spare not—
So send I you to taste of Calvary.

—*E. Margaret Clarkson.*

Oh, let us remember that God takes the part of His servants and comes to the help of those who trust Him. And so we remember:

"Let your conversation be without covetousness; and be content with such things as ye have: for he hath said, I will never leave thee, nor forsake thee. So that we may boldly say, The Lord is my helper, and I will not fear what man shall do unto me."— Heb. 13:5,6.

III. With Moses on Mount Nebo:
Good-By Israel

We stand on Mount Nebo, a peak of the mountains of Moab, east of the Jordan River, "over against Jericho," as the Bible says. Here is where Moses was brought to look over the land of Canaan which he could not enter. Near here God buried him and "no man knoweth of his sepulchre unto this day" (Deut. 34:6).

Because Moses lost his temper and did not honor God in the matter of smiting the rock instead of speaking to it for water for the Israelites, he was not allowed to go into Palestine proper. He must die here.

Our hearts are deeply stirred as we face with Moses this closing of a life's work and looking hungrily into the land which he could not enter until he would come down with Elijah to meet Jesus on the Mount of Transfiguration!

Let's See the Countries Around Mount Nebo

We are now in the Hashemite kingdom of Jordan, with the capital city being Amman. But in Bible times this lower part of Jordan was occupied by the Moabites. North of us is the country of the Ammonites. The name comes down to us in Amman, the name of the capital city of Jordan now. But the city was called Rabbah in David's time. It was there Joab and the army were besieging the city when David sinned with Bathsheba. We saw the citadel the other day and drove up on it. It was there that Uriah the Hittite was put close to the wall at David's order and was killed.

Jordan has King Hussein. He was educated in England, and is

friendly to the United States. The people are Arabs and are principally Moslem.

North of Jordan is Syria. The capital of Syria is Damascus, the
oldest continuously inhabited city in the world. Syrians were
often great enemies of Israel, and are so today. Abraham had as
chief servant Eliezer who was from Damascus. Naaman was a
Syrian general, greatly used in his country but with leprosy. He
was healed by dipping, as Elijah commanded, seven times in the
River Jordan.

South of these mountains of Moab is Edom, the country of
Esau's people and the Rose Red city of Petra cut out in stone.
Further south still and west toward Sinai Peninsula and toward
Egypt were the hosts of the Midianites.

From Jaresh north of Amman, our three buses drove nearly
two hundred miles south to the resort town of Aqaba at the head
of the Gulf of Aqaba, an arm of the Red Sea. This was the Bible
port of Ezion Geber from whence Solomon's ships sailed to bring
back gold from Ophir; ivory, apes and peacocks, from Africa.
Four nations reaching the head of this gulf are within a few miles
of each other—Egypt, Israel, Jordan and Saudi Arabia. We
stayed in the new Holiday Inn overnight, looked on the many
ships in the big port, including battleships.

The next morning we drove to Petra and rode horses through
the narrow valley and saw the buildings cut in stone. Then we
went to Mount Nebo where all of our three buses unloaded
together and I preached to our crowd looking across the Jordan
and the Dead Sea with the mountain breezes in our hair!

How our souls burned within us as we envisioned Moses, 120
years old, still strong and vigorous, but saying good-by to all his
dreams and plans about Palestine!

I. MOSES, LAY DOWN YOUR BURDENS!

I cannot but think it was more mercy than judgment for God to
take Moses home to Heaven. Indeed, he has done his part. Safe
from Egypt he has brought the nation, perhaps three million
strong. He has given the law of God, the ceremonies, the
priesthood, the sacrifices. He has borne these rebellious,

childish, backsliding Israelites as a father training a child. Lay down your burden, Moses!

1. A Nation Has Been Delivered From Slavery!

It was his dream as a little child to deliver Israel. He was nursed by his mother, a paid maid to the princess, Pharaoh's daughter. He surely must have been taught to love Israel, his people. He must have been taught to grieve over their slavery. One day he decided to forsake all the comforts and riches and position of Egypt to be God's man, "choosing rather to suffer affliction with the people of God, than to enjoy the pleasures of sin for a season; Esteeming the reproach of Christ greater riches than the treasures in Egypt" (Heb. 11:25,26). He dreamed he must deliver Israel.

He boldly killed an Egyptian who oppressed an Israelite and was shocked to find the Israelites would not hear him when he wanted to free them. He fled for his life.

He dwelt forty years in the backside of the desert of Midian. When he had at last lost his assurance, we believe, and when he was eighty years old, surely, now it was too late to deliver Israel. But God called him. He gave him great promises, put His blessing on the rod in Moses' hand. He was so fearful, yet he went and grew in boldness as God revealed His power.

Great plagues were brought upon Egypt—water turned to blood, the frogs, the flies, the lice, the hail from Heaven, the locusts, the midnight darkness, and then the death angel who took every firstborn son where there was no blood on the door. At last, then, they could leave Egypt. When the armies pursued them, God opened the Red Sea and destroyed the armies of Pharaoh.

God sent them a heavenly light, a pillar of fire, to guide them and be between them and Pharaoh's army. It was a pillar of cloud by day and through forty years it did not leave them. Manna fell from Heaven, angel food, to feed the multitude day after day, week after week, month after month, year after year, for forty years! What deliverance, Moses! Lay down your burden. Israel is free and ready to enter into the Promised Land, that land flowing with milk and honey.

2. Moses, You Have Given the Law With Its Priesthood, Offerings, Ceremonies and Commands of God

Israel has the law you have given. You went forty days in fasting and again forty days in the presence of God on Mount Sinai. Your face shone as you came down from that mountain. You received not only the Ten Commandments but the Sabbath, the priesthood, the offerings. You received and recorded all the instructions of the law. You saw the heavenly pattern of the tabernacle with its brazen altar, with the table of shewbread, with the golden lampstand, with the altar of incense. You saw God's holy of holies and the ark of the covenant that you would prepare therein and the cherubims overshadowing it. You wrote down the moral standards that would be forever the basis of morality and laws as long as civilized nations endure.

Moses, you saw more miracles than all the other men of the Old or New Testaments except those of Jesus Christ. You wrote down far more Scripture given from God than any other man who ever lived. Paul's fourteen letters make only 75 pages in the Bible without notes, to you 190 pages for the Pentateuch. Add the five books by John and two by Luke, and still more Scripture was given through your pen than through these twenty-one books in the New Testament. Oh, Moses, the mighty man of God, lay down your burden! How much the world owes to you! Do not fret that you now are to go Home.

3. Moses, You Have Preserved and Grown a Nation

They were slaves in Egypt. Now they are a nation of free men, the most enlightened and favored on earth. You carried them as a nursing father carries a baby in his bosom.

You stood in the gap when God would have destroyed them. When God suggested He would blot out this rebellious nation and take you and your family to start again the promised nation of Israel, you refused.

You rebuked the people. You loved them. You prayed for them. You punished them and asked God to punish them when it was necessary.

You saw Miriam made a leper for a time because of her rebellion. You saw the earth open to swallow up the tents and the peo-

ple of Dathan and Abiram, and they went down alive into the
pit. When Israel made a golden calf and danced naked and
drunken around it, you called, "Who is on the Lord's side?
let him come unto me." And the swords of God's vengeance slew
many that day. Oh, you were strict and sharp, but how lovingly
and how patiently you carried Israel as a babe in arms and made
them into a nation!

You taught the people, you loved them, you rebuked them,
you prayed for them. You made the mob of slaves into a civilized,
moral nation. Now, Moses, lay down your burdens. You are an
old man. Joshua will lead. God will keep His promises. The
Christ you know of will come in time to the land of Canaan. Lay
down your heavy burdens and rest in the arms of God.

II. THE LAND YOU SEE, MOSES, IS DEAR TO GOD

Moses' eyes were not dimmed nor his strength abated, we are
told, although he was 120 years old. Looking from Mount Nebo,
he saw "unto the utmost sea," that is, over the Jordan River,
over the wilderness of Judaea, over the mountains, the Plain of
Sharon, even to the Mediterranean Sea. He saw the area to be
given to each tribe. It may be that God helped him to see more
than we could see standing there.

The day was hazy as we stood on Mount Nebo. We could see
the dim form of the Mount of Olives, perhaps thirty miles away.
Jerusalem was just below and beyond it. Below us the Jordan
showed as a strip of green. The Dead Sea looked like a small lake
seen from the mountain top.

1. This Is the Land Promised to Abraham

Abraham was to walk through the land. Look north, east,
south and west; all the land of Canaan, God promised in Genesis
13:14-17, was to be his. It was to Abraham and his seed—first of
all, to the literal descendants of Abraham, Isaac and Jacob. Four
hundred and thirty years have gone by, Moses, besides the forty
years in the wilderness since Abraham was a sojourner in
Palestine. Over two hundred years Israel was in Egypt. Now the
"land flowing with milk and honey" will belong to Israel, the
children of Abraham. God's promise to Abraham was "for ever"

(Gen. 13:15). So God can devastate the country by war, can restore it in the millennium, can purge it with fire as II Peter 3:7 foretells, but the land will not pass away. Abraham and his seed have eternal title to it.

2. This Is the Land of David's Kingdom

God promised David a kingly line. In II Samuel 7:10-16 is this promise:

"Moreover I will appoint a place for my people Israel, and will plant them, that they may dwell in a place of their own, and move no more; neither shall the children of wickedness afflict them any more, as beforetime, And as since the time that I commanded judges to be over my people Israel, and have caused thee to rest from all thine enemies. Also the Lord telleth thee that he will make thee an house. And when thy days be fulfilled, and thou shalt sleep with thy fathers, I will set up thy seed after thee, which shall proceed out of thy bowels, and I will establish his kingdom. He shall build an house for my name, and I will stablish the throne of his kingdom for ever. I will be his father, and he shall be my son. If he commit iniquity, I will chasten him with the rod of men, and with the stripes of the children of men: But my mercy shall not depart away from him, as I took it from Saul, whom I put away before thee. And thine house and thy kingdom shall be established for ever before thee: thy throne shall be established for ever."

Note that the promise is future. Not "I have" but "I *will* appoint a place." It is some future time. No more captivity in Babylon, no more destruction of Jerusalem as in A. D. 70. "And thine house and thy kingdom *shall be* established for ever before thee: thy throne *shall* be established for ever." Not at once with Solomon. No, far later—with Jesus, the Son of David, as He returns to sit on David's throne. For to the virgin Mary the Angel Gabriel promised, "the Lord God shall give unto him the throne of his father David: And he shall reign over the house of Jacob for ever" (Luke 1:32,33). Solomon will fall into idolatry, the kingdom for a time will decay and be laid aside, but from his brother Nathan will come the line through which the Saviour will come, as we learn in the genealogy of Luke 3.

3. But This Will Be the Land of the Lord Jesus

Moses, you saw it ahead of time, for Jesus said later that Moses "wrote of me" (John 5:46). You wrote down how the Seed of the woman would crush the serpent's head. You saw the time coming when "the Lord thy God will raise up unto thee a Prophet from the midst of thee, of thy brethren, like unto me; unto him ye shall hearken" (Deut. 18:15). Again you reported what God said, "I will raise them up a Prophet from among their brethren, like unto thee, and will put my words in his mouth; and he shall speak unto them all that I shall command him" (Deut. 18:18).

You knew that the passover lamb, male of the first year, without blemish, killed each fourteenth day of Nisan, pictured the Lamb of God, the end of all sacrifices. Yes, in this land Palestine, in the fullness of time, the Saviour, the Creator, the first begotten of God physically, will be born of a virgin at Bethlehem. He will live the perfect life, a second Adam. He will speak as "never man spake" and will at last die on Mount Moriah as Abraham's offering of Isaac pictured. There His precious blood poured out, not the blood of bulls and goats but the precious blood of Christ, will pay for man's sin and then Christ will rise again. He will set men to preaching the Gospel in all the world and then ascend back into Heaven. And it will be as the land of Jesus.

4. Yes, Moses, and Canaan Will Be the Center of Christ's Millennial Kingdom

It is true that Israel, the nation of Jews, is the seed of Abraham according to the flesh. But one of the promises of God was to Abraham and his Seed—not seeds, plural—but one Seed, Christ (Gal. 3:16). So it is Christ who will come to reign in that wonderful time when "the earth shall be filled with the knowledge of the glory of the Lord, as the waters cover the sea," the time when "the eyes of the blind shall be opened, and the ears of the deaf shall be unstopped. Then shall the lame man leap as an hart." Oh, happy time, when Christ comes back to reign on the earth!

The promise about Christ's coming was not simply the first

time but it will be completed another time. Jesus must sit on the throne of His father David. The time must come as foretold in Isaiah, chapter 7, when there will come a sprout from the root of David. The kingly line will be established again and Christ will reign in the power of God. At that time the Scripture says, ". . . and the Lord shall be king over all the earth: in that day . . ." (Zech. 14:9).

> Sorrow and sighing shall flee away,
> When Jesus comes to reign.
> Eyes of the blind will be opened then;
> Tongue of the dumb shall sing.
>
> Raptured with Christ, then a honeymoon
> With Him in gloryland,
> With Him to earth, when the angels bring
> Israel to Holy land.
>
> Lame men shall leap as an hart, for then
> All sickness gone, all sore.
> Deserts will bloom and the thorns, and briars
> Shall curse the earth no more!
>
> Kingdoms shall fall, and old Satan's rule
> Shall end with all its tears.
> Righteousness fill all the earth, and peace
> Reign for a thousand years.
>
> We pray, dear Lord, may Thy Kingdom come,
> On earth Thy will be done.
> But we have now all Thy peace and joy
> And in our hearts Thy throne.
>
> Sorrow and sighing shall flee away!
> Flee away that glory day!
> Garden of Eden restored that day!
> When Jesus comes to reign.

III. MOSES, CONSIDER THE FUTURE OF YOUR PEOPLE ISRAEL

I do not suppose that any man ever lived in all the history of Israel who loved that nation of people more than Moses did. Now, Moses, consider what God has in mind for this people. You will not get to lead them into the land of Canaan but Joshua will lead them.

1. They Will Grow Into a Great Nation

First, there is the period of conquest, the great blessings, the fall of Jericho, and then, bit by bit, the conquering of most of the land under Joshua's great leadership. How good God was!

Then there comes a period of judges. The people sin and God brings fresh punishment and they repent; God raises up some judge to deliver them.

Then the people will cry out for a king and God will allow them to have King Saul. But Saul does not meticulously follow the Lord, and at last God raises up David, the son of Jesse, to be king over Israel. What greatness came to the nation as David's kingdom expanded everywhere! And David would lay by millions of dollars to be put into a great Temple which his son Solomon would build. What a kingdom!

2. But, Moses, There Will Come Idolatry and Worldliness

The people will forget God. Solomon will fall into idolatry. The nation will be divided in two. Then, first, the Northern Kingdom will be carried captive by the Assyrians, then Nebuchadnezzar will come at last and destroy Jerusalem and take away the choicest of all the people of Israel to Babylon.

Seventy years will go by while the land "enjoys her sabbaths," those Sabbaths that were neglected and violated through the years and now made good. And then God will raise up a remnant under Ezra and under Nehemiah. They will come back to Palestine and build again a Temple and then the walls of Jerusalem and Israel will be a nation again.

Then the Saviour will come, born at Bethlehem, live at Capernaum, preach in Galilee and come again and again to Jerusalem. And at long last the nation Israel has her chance at the Saviour.

3. But Christ Will Be Rejected by the People

He will pronounce a curse on Chorazin, on Bethsaida, on Capernaum, where most of His mighty works are done. He will promise the destruction of Jerusalem and the Temple left desolate. And Christ will die and then in about the year A. D. 70, Titus, with the Roman army, will come to besiege Jerusalem and put down the rebellion of the Zealots. Jerusalem will be leveled to the ground and Israel scattered to all the world.

And they are still scattered. They are still the same rebellious people rejecting the Saviour like their fathers who rejected Him and brought the curse on the nation before.

It is true, a group of Zionists have gone back to Jerusalem and there is a little nation there. We wish them well, but that is not the restoration of Israel that is promised. That is not the fulfillment of promise. Israel has not turned back to God. Still the hand of God in punishment is on the nation until they return to the Saviour.

4. Oh, But Christ Will One Day Restore Israel!

We are told that after the tribulation of those days that Christ will return in clouds of glory. He will send His angels to regather His elect, His people Israel from every store, bank, fire sale and business. He will gather from all the world every Jew left alive. And Ezekiel 10:34-38 tells us they will be taken back to the wilderness of wanderings and there the rebels will be purged out. And Zechariah 12 and 13 tells us how "they shall look upon me whom they have pierced," and they will say, "What are these wounds in thine hands?" Oh, then the nation with the rebels purged out will repent, every family apart, as one mourns for his firstborn son. "So all Israel shall be saved," Romans 11:26 says.

What a grand time of revival when the blindness that is now in the eyes of Israel will be taken away; when they shall see their Saviour and return to Him. And then the battle of Armageddon will take place. God will destroy His enemies and set up the kingdom of Christ on earth. And then Israel will come into her own, that is, the remnant of Israel, those who love and trust the Saviour.

Moses, lay down your burden. You have had a full life. You are an old man. Now go to rest in the arms of God and wait until these things shall be fulfilled. And one day, Moses, you and the Prophet Elijah will come together to the Mount of Transfiguration and there you will talk with Jesus and discuss "his decease which he should accomplish at Jerusalem." Until that time, Moses, rest in the promises and rejoice in the great God so dear to you. You will have your chance at Palestine again.

IV. At Bethlehem Where Jesus Was Born

How my spirit quickens within me as we near Bethlehem, the birthplace of the Saviour. So many fragrant memories of Bible personalities and events cluster around this little city, six miles southwest of Jerusalem. As we near the city, there is the tomb said to be the burial place of Rachel who died giving birth to Benjamin: "And Rachel died, and was buried in the way to Ephrath, which is Beth-lehem" (Gen. 35:19).

Bethlehem was the home town of Naomi. To here she returned after she sojourned in Moab and lost her husband and two sons. With her came the beloved daughter-in-law Ruth. Here was the field of Boaz where Ruth came to glean, and Boaz respected and loved the young woman, took her as his wife, and so she entered into the ancestral line of the Saviour, to bear Obed, the father of Jesse, and grandfather of King David.

Bethlehem was the home of David. Once, a little homesick out yonder in war, he said, "Oh that one would give me drink of the water of the well of Beth-lehem. . . ." And two of his warriors broke through the Philistine lines and got the drink of water for David. But he would not drink this, which was like the blood of these men who loved him, so he poured it out before the Lord (II Sam. 23:15,16).

Ah, but mainly Bethlehem is beloved and precious because here the Saviour was born!

It was foretold in Micah 5:2, "But thou, Beth-lehem Ephratah, though thou be little among the thousands of Judah, yet out of thee shall he come forth unto me that is to be ruler in Israel; whose goings forth have been from of old, from everlasting." Jesus, the Messiah, must be born here.

But Mary, the virgin who is to bear the Saviour, lived at Nazareth, about a hundred miles away! And she is engaged to marry Joseph the carpenter who lives there! How will the Saviour be born in Bethlehem?

Oh, that is no problem for God, for "the earth is the Lord's, and the fulness thereof; the world, and they that dwell therein." So God had Caesar Augustus at Rome pass a rule that everybody must go back to his ancestral home to register for taxation. Mary is of the house and lineage of David and so is Joseph, so they must go back to Bethlehem, the home of David, to register.

In Luke 2:1-7 we read:

"And it came to pass in those days, that there went out a decree from Caesar Augustus, that all the world should be taxed. (And this taxing was first made when Cyrenius was governor of Syria.) And all went to be taxed, every one unto his own city. And Joseph also went up from Galilee, out of the city of Nazareth, into Judaea, unto the city of David, which is called Bethlehem; (because he was of the house and lineage of David:) To be taxed. with Mary his espoused wife, being great with child. And so it was, that, while they were there, the days were accomplished that she should be delivered. And she brought forth her firstborn son, and wrapped him in swaddling clothes, and laid him in a manger; because there was no room for them in the inn."

Nearby here is the Field of the Shepherds where they heard the angel's announcement and rejoiced and came to see the Baby Jesus. They were told, "For unto you is born this day in the city of David a Saviour, which is Christ the Lord" (vs. 11).

The Wise Men came to see the Baby Jesus here, having seen His star in the East. They probably had read the prophecy of Daniel and counted the 283 years to the coming of the Saviour, 69 weeks of years (Dan. 9:25).

Phillips Brooks, the great Episcopal preacher, wrote

O LITTLE TOWN OF BETHLEHEM

O little town of Bethlehem,
  How still we see thee lie!
Above thy deep and dreamless sleep
  The silent stars go by;
Yet in thy dark streets shineth
  The everlasting Light;
The hopes and fears of all the years
  Are met in thee tonight.

For Christ is born of Mary;
  And gathered all above,
While mortals sleep, the angels keep
  Their watch of wond'ring love.
O morning stars, together
  Proclaim the holy birth,
And praises sing to God the King,
  And peace to men on earth.

How silently, how silently
  The wondrous gift is giv'n!
So God imparts to human hearts
  The blessings of His Heav'n.
No ear may hear His coming;
  But in this world of sin,
Where meek souls will receive Him still,
  The dear Christ enters in.

O holy Child of Bethlehem,
  Descend to us, we pray;
Cast out our sin and enter in,
  Be born in us today.
We hear the Christmas angels
  The great glad tidings tell,—
O come to us, abide with us,
  Our Lord Emmanuel!

Here the Saviour was born. Here came Wise Men from the
East to see the Baby. They opened their treasures to Him—gold,
frankincense and myrrh. Herod would have killed the Baby but
they were warned of God in a dream—the Wise Men went back
another way and Joseph and Mary fled to Egypt where the Child
was safe until the death of Herod.

Oh, Bethlehem has many implications for the earnest Chris-

Church of the Nativity over the cave selected by
Queen Helena about 324 A.D.

tian. I have always been glad to see it on my many tours of Bible lands.

I. WE VISIT THE CAVE WHICH TRADITION NAMES AS THE BIRTHPLACE

We come to Bethlehem from Jerusalem and a large square is left for parking the many sight-seeing buses which come daily. And we are at once besieged by salesmen who want to sell us slides, necklaces of olive wood or postcards.

1. The Church of the Nativity

The Church of the Nativity has been built over the cave which is the supposed site of the Saviour's birth. It has the usual floor plan and columns of a bisilica. Once it was entered by a roomy arched door. But we are told that Moslem people and soldiers felt free to ride into the church on their horses or camels, so the arch was largely filled up and now one bows low to enter a door about four feet high. We suppose it is intended to remind people to be humble!

Inside the guide tells us that this church was built after a former building was destroyed. And he shows us a mosaic remnant of that floor a few inches lower than the present floor. This large Roman Catholic church building is adjoined by other buildings used by Greek Orthodox Catholic, Armenian Catholics, etc. The site for the church was selected about 324 A.D., when Queen Helena, the mother of Emperor Constantine, came to Palestine at about the age of 80 to select a place for the church to celebrate the birth of Christ, one at Nazareth to memorialize the announcement to Mary, one at Jerusalem to represent the place of the crucifixion and burial of Jesus. There are no seats in the church, and, we suppose, no preaching services, but Mass is conducted occasionally. Priests care for the building and for the cave underneath.

2. The Cave Itself

We enter by descending concrete steps. One is a little disappointed to find that all the interior has been relined or covered and part of the cave is partitioned off. There is a spot with a mosaic and a star, representing, we are told, the very spot where the Baby Jesus was born. Then there is a little niche which we are told was the manger where He was laid.

And hanging from the wall are many, many ornate and expensive lamps, given here by kings and rulers of many states in the days before electricity lighted the cave. When we have had our little service with our tour group in which we tell the story of the coming of Mary and Joseph and the fact that there was no room in the inn and the Baby laid in a manger, and then we tell them how the place was selected by Queen Helena, we sing "Silent Night," and depart out another stairway into the adjacent church.

Here, in a section of this same cave, now partitioned off, Jerome translated the *Latin Vulgate,* which was for centuries the version of the Bible from which other Catholic versions were translated in other languages. It was prepared here by Jerome from original Greek and Latin. He lived in the cave and worked here.

Tradition says also that in this cave they cast the bodies of the boy babies who were killed at Herod's command, trying to destroy the Baby Jesus. There is no evidence for that.

II. IS THIS CAVE ACTUALLY THE BIRTHPLACE OF THE LORD JESUS?

We think it doubtful for several reasons.

1. It Is Three Hundred Years Too Late

This was designated as the birthplace of Jesus only after more than 300 years. Queen Helena, mother of Emperor Constantine, who had become nominally a Christian at least, and she, we suppose, a devout Christian, came to the Holy Land in the years 324 A. D. to 327 A.D. She selected this place as the birthplace of the Saviour.

How could she find such a place?

We will remember that Jerusalem was destroyed in A.D. 70 and the whole country was devastated and the Jews were killed or sold into slavery or scattered to all the world. In Jerusalem not one stone was left upon another in the Temple. It is certain that

Within the cave: Left: marks the place somebody decided was the birth spot. To the right: supposed location of the manger.

Jewish people of all the nation were the victims of this terrible destruction brought on by the revolt of the Zealots. It is certain that after 300 years there would be no reputable witnesses who knew where the birthplace of Jesus was. The simple truth is that after Jesus was born, in a few days He was spirited away to Egypt and there was no reason why local inhabitants would mark especially the place of His birth. Joseph and Mary were poor ignorant peasants with no money. They left soon. Jesus was not recognized as the Saviour by the people generally. And no one marked the place.

Again, it seems likely there would be no house standing that could have been the birthplace of Jesus after 324 years. Our nation America is only 200 years old this year, yet the birthplace of obscure people who did not become famous or well known until long later can rarely be found or identified. There is no way I could find the house where I was born. I went back when I was twelve years old or more to see the little house where we lived when my father was pastor of a country church near Gainesville,

Texas, but the house had been destroyed.

Some years ago I went back to the ranch to which we moved when I was nine years old. That ranch house, which had been the headquarters for six thousand acres, was gone, either moved or destroyed.

Why would you suppose that anyone would know how to designate the very house or the very place where Jesus was born?

That meant that Queen Helena had to go on some fleeting impression of her own and not on any facts in the case. No house was a prospect, we suppose, so she chose a cave as the place of Jesus' birth.

2. The Bible Says Nothing About Jesus Being Born in a Cave

Luke 2:6,7 tells about the birth of Christ as follows:

"And so it was, that, while they were there, the days were accomplished that she should be delivered. And she brought forth her firstborn son, and wrapped him in swaddling clothes, and laid him in a manger; because there was no room for them in the inn."

Where were they staying? Somewhere in a stable, or perhaps camping out under the stars. The city was full because of the great host of people descended from King David. So she wrapped the Baby "in swaddling clothes, and laid him in a manger; because there was no room for them in the inn." We do not know where the manger was. Probably it was a manger adjacent to the inn where there was found no room for them.

The Baby Jesus in Bethlehem is mentioned again in Matthew, chapter 2, where the Wise Men came from the East to see Him. They first inquired in Jerusalem, and learned that the Saviour was to be born in Bethlehem, according to Micah 5:2. As they came to Jerusalem they saw the star. They came to Bethlehem "and, lo, the star, which they saw in the east, went before them, till it came and stood over where the young child was. When they saw the star, they rejoiced with exceeding great joy. And when they were come into the house, they saw the young child with Mary his mother, and fell down, and worshipped him."

They came "into the house." There is no mention here of a cave. So it is presumptuous to claim that there must be a cave.

3. God Seems to Have Deliberately Hidden the Exact Place From Us

There is a great frailty in the human heart. We look for the incidentals instead of the fundamentals. Men want to reverence places, houses, men, instead of God. Men call the church auditorium "the sanctuary," which it is not. The only temple God has on earth is now the body of the Christian. They want to "reverence the house of God" instead of God and the Gospel. So we must take particular caution not to make more of incidental object lessons than God intended.

The Lord had Moses make a brazen serpent and set it on a pole so the snake-bitten Israelites could look to that, and looking, by faith could be healed. And they were. That snake on a pole was a reminder of Jesus who will be hanged on a cross and there will bear our sins and be counted a sinner in our place. But it turned out that after that wonderful demonstration of the Gospel in the Old Testament and people healed, as told in Numbers 21:5-9, then people put up that brass serpent and it became an idol.

Later, when there came a great revival under King Hezekiah, "He removed the high places, and brake the images, and cut down the groves, and brake in pieces the brasen serpent that Moses had made: for unto those days the children of Israel did burn incense to it: and he called it Nehushtan" (II Kings 18:4). That brazen object which was intended for a wonderful spiritual lesson had been used as an idol.

Some people would make baptism, a beautiful ordinance which pictures the burial and resurrection of Christ and the believer's burial of the old sinner to live a new life, an idol and put that as part of the plan of salvation! Or the Lord's Supper, which is simply a memorial reminding us again of the death of Christ, is used as if it actually became a sacrifice to make a "means of grace" to those who take it.

Why is it that the Crusaders who sought so earnestly for the "holy grail," the cup with which the Lord had given the Last Supper, could never find it? Because that cup is of no importance to God nor to us, and God does not want us worshiping things. There is no way to find the two stones upon which were engraved the Ten Commandments with the finger of God; no finding of the golden lampstand, candlestick, from the Temple.

So when we come to Palestine, we find that God has left indefinite and unproven the sites which people would like to know. Was Jesus born in this cave at Bethlehem? We do not know. Does the Church of the Holy Sepulchre at Jerusalem actually cover the site of the crucifixion, burial and resurrection? It does not seem likely. That crucifixion was "outside the camp." It was "near the city." And that cleverly fabricated sepulchre of marble in that Church of the Holy Sepulchre does not appear to be, and could not be, the tomb cut out of the solid rock where Joseph of Arimathaea laid the body of Jesus.

You say multitudes think that is the place. Yes, and other multitudes think the hill Calvary above the Garden Tomb is the place of the crucifixion, and the Garden Tomb the place of burial. We do not know. God did not intend people to worship these places.

Does anyone know just where the angel appeared to Mary to announce the birth of the Saviour? Certainly not. Men would like to know. But God wants people to rejoice in the great historical fact that Christ came and died for us and arose again, and He does not want the devotion to be placed on things, places, relics and ceremonies. This principle that God seems to hide things that might tempt us to idolatry adds to the evidence that perhaps the cave was not where Jesus was born. And Jesus often spoke deliberately in parables so the truth would be revealed to the earnest, seeking heart but hidden from those who did not much care.

III. OH, BUT WE KNOW JESUS WAS BORN IN BETHLEHEM!

We cannot be sure that in a certain little spot in a cave the Saviour was born. But what does that matter? We know He was born there!

1. Rejoice in the Saviour's Birth

It is far more important that—as I stood in that cave and sang, "Silent Night, Holy Night"—far more important that I knew Christ is in my heart and in my body than that one time the Baby Jesus lay in a manger nearby. I do not know where. But the Lord Jesus was born. And He is my Saviour.

Someone argued with another, "I believe Jesus was crucified and buried down at the site of the Church of the Holy Sepulchre." Another said, "No, I believe He was crucified and buried in Joseph's new tomb in the place called Gordon's Calvary and buried in the new tomb under that hill, in the Garden Tomb."

But what does it matter? I have been both places and wherever it was, Jesus is risen and gone. He was not at either place. He lives today!

We can sing sweet songs about the birth of Jesus and about Bethlehem, for Jesus was born and Bethlehem is a reminder of it. Oh, wonderful fact that God became Man, that Jesus came into this world through the same portals as all others of mankind, took on Himself all the burdens and trials and temptations of the human race, then the sinless Saviour died in my place and rose again.

Let us not forget that Christ was born in Bethlehem, and never mind too much about what exact spot.

2. Nearby Is the Field of the Shepherds

Is the field now called the Field of the Shepherds the very place where the angels came and where the sky was filled with glory and where the angel said, "Fear not: for, behold, I bring you good tidings of great joy, which shall be to all people"? Is this the place? And was that field lighted with the glory of Heaven as a multitude of angels chanted, "Glory to God in the highest, and on earth peace, good will toward men"? I think it may be. It was nearby.

Oh, but never mind about the exact spot. The angel did appear. He did give those glad tidings which shall be for all people, and that Saviour is my Saviour and He is alive today! He is as real to me as to those shepherds who hurried that day to see the Baby in a manger.

Is that field called the Shepherd's Field the same field that belonged to Boaz? Is that where Ruth the Moabitess girl, with a love for the God of Israel, who had come to rest under His wings, gleaned and where she came and lay at the feet of Boaz, and where he fell in love with her and took her to be his wife so that they, too, were in the ancestral line of the Saviour? I think it may be.

The Shepherd's Field, Bethlehem

The Shepherd's Field, Bethlehem

And is it true that somewhere near here the boy David found a lion seizing a lamb of the flock and he, with great boldness and the power of God, seized that lion by his beard and slew him? I think so; it was somewhere near here, at least. We have the Bible and it is true, and all this land is a holy land, whether we can locate identical spots or not.

Our Catholic friends had a great custom of building a church over every place of some historical, biblical significance. To me, that someway takes away from the beauty of the places. One young college girl who went with us on the tour of the Holy Land sat down and wept, saying, "They have ruined it all!" She could not see things as they had been when Jesus was here because of the churches built in Bethlehem, in Jerusalem, in the Garden of Gethsemane, in Nazareth and elsewhere. I said rather facetiously, "I am glad to find they haven't built a church yet over the Sea of Galilee."

But, thank God, we have all the historical truth, and we have the Person of Christ and the blessed, wonderful history of it all in the eternal Word of God.

Here is my little Christmas song:

JESUS, BABY JESUS

Jesus, Baby Jesus, of a virgin mother born,
Laid in manger cradle, wrapped in swaddling clothes and warm.
Birth cry in a darkened stable, in the inn no room.
Jesus, Baby Jesus, Son of God, to share earth's gloom.

Jesus, how the angels with delight the story told,
Told to Mary, Joseph and the shepherds at their fold.
Full of light, the heavens, as they chanted "peace on earth"!
Jesus, Baby Jesus, what glad news, a Saviour's birth!

Wise men came to see Him, having seen His star afar,
Bro't their gifts of precious gold and frankincense and myrrh.
Herod heard, was troubled, could not kill the holy Child.
Jesus, Baby Jesus, King and Priest, and Saviour mild.

Jesus, Baby Jesus, Son of God and Son of Man,
Tempted, poor and suff'ring, no one knows us as He can!
Holy, righteous, blameless, fitting sacrifice complete.
By His blood atonement, God and sinners in Him meet.

Jesus, Baby Jesus,
There's a cross along the way.
Born to die for sinners,
Born for crucifixion day!

V. *In Nazareth Where Jesus Grew Up*

The little town of Nazareth is about 75 or 80 miles north of Jerusalem, and 15 miles west of the Sea of Galilee. We go north from Jerusalem, up and down hills, by Shechem and by Jacob's Well. We might turn, perhaps, and go to the Hill Samaria, which was the site of the capital of Northern Israel when Ahab was king. We will stop, perhaps, at the village of Sebastia to see on that hill the ruins of Ahab's palace and the Herodian Temple. Then we will go on north through the Valley of Megiddo, past the tel or mound where the ancient fortress is being excavated and where Solomon stationed hundreds of his chariots and horses. They were there to defend this great valley from any invasion coming from the north and east around the Fertile Crescent.

It is in that valley where will occur the giant battle of Armageddon foretold in Revelation 16:16. Then the armies of the Antichrist, 200 million strong, devil-possessed men, will be destroyed by Christ Jesus and His armies from Heaven. Their blood will run to the bridles of the horses. That is before Christ sets up His kingdom but after He returns to reign on the earth.

We go on past Mount Tabor which is thought to be the Mount of Transfiguration and then up the hills to Nazareth. We pass the hill called the "Hill of Precipitation" and go into the little town of Nazareth itself.

I. LET US LEARN ABOUT NAZARETH

Nazareth is an Arab town, and here you will find some Arabs

with donkeys carrying loads, as well as trucks and cars. The population is about 40,000. A newer Jewish community overlooks the old town, built further on the hills.

1. Important Events That Make Nazareth Sacred to Many

It was here that the Angel Gabriel appeared to Mary and announced that she would be the mother of the Saviour. Oh, what a startling event that the first time in all God's history God Himself would beget and have a Son born of a virgin! And to Mary it was explained that the Holy Spirit would come upon her and she would be the mother of the Saviour.

It was here, too, where Mary and Joseph returned to live after they had been to Bethlehem where the Baby Jesus was born, after they had fled from Herod to Egypt in fear, for he would destroy the Baby Jesus; but when Herod was dead, they came back and lived in Nazareth. It was here Joseph had his carpenter shop; here Jesus, no doubt, worked with him in the carpenter shop and lived His sinless, blameless life before the time came for His showing to the world.

Here Jesus lived, after His return from Egypt as a Baby, until He was thirty years old and ready to begin His ministry. And after He was baptized, He moved to Capernaum, on the Sea of Galilee.

It was here Jesus returned after He was preaching wonderfully and reported that now He was filled with the Spirit and the Scriptures are fulfilled.

2. Here Is the Church of the Annunciation

Queen Helena, the mother of Emperor Constantine, came to Palestine in the year 324 A.D. and in Nazareth she selected a place which she designated as a site where the angel appeared to Mary. And there they built the Church of the Annunciation. It was near a cave where they said was Joseph's carpenter shop as well as the home of Joseph and Mary.

Now the old church had a baptistry for immersion, and that is not surprising. So did all the Catholic churches up to the thirteenth century. Then Catholic leaders decided that baptism was essential to salvation and it was easier to sprinkle than to immerse, so they officially changed from immersion to sprinkling. As they had changed the meaning, so they changed the form. And the old church had still the baptistry for immersion. It was true also in the Church of Saint John in Ephesus, the ruins of which we have seen.

Now that church in Nazareth has been replaced by a great Catholic church building. We are told that the money for it was raised by the pope himself and inside it great areas are provided by the gifts of faithful Catholics around the world in many nations.

3. Is This the Authentic Site of the Angel's Appearance to Mary?

Like many Catholic traditions, the announced place of the annunciation is suspect. There is no evidence to support it. It was evidently a woman's idea, decided so good people would have a place to reverence, and so it was thought their devotion would be increased. But there are many things that make us question whether this is the site.

First, nothing in Scripture indicates in what part of Nazareth the angel appeared. Then you must remember that nearly all Palestine was devastated in the wars by Titus in A.D. 70 when Jerusalem was destroyed. And the last armies of the Zealot Jews at Masada held out three years longer. As far as we know, the great area of Palestine was devastated and houses were burned, the people were killed or sold into slavery, and so there would be no record, and no one would live who remembered 300 years before where an angel had appeared to Mary. When Queen Helena came 324 years after the birth of Christ, it was too late for her to find where an angel had appeared to Mary. Besides, who would know about it but Mary? She did not mark the place and there is no record of it.

No, we do not believe the cave over which the Church of the Annunciation was built is where the angel appeared to Mary. We must remember that God seemed to have a way of hiding some things from us where people would be likely to worship things and places instead of rejoicing in the great scriptural event that happened.

A well in Nazareth is called the Virgin's Fountain or Mary's Well. Why? Because in old times it was the only well in Nazareth

Nazareth: in the center the new Church of the Annunciation

and women came there to get their pitchers of water. No doubt
Mary, like others, got water at that well, but it was not in any
particular sense connected with Mary.

But Nazareth was where Jesus grew to manhood, and I love to
walk about the place and remember that Jesus was here for
many years, walking up and down these streets or other streets
like them, long ago.

II. MARY, THE VIRGIN MOTHER

I can imagine that Mary was a modest and spiritually-minded
young woman who lived a clean and wholesome life.

1. She Was to Bear the Saviour

The angel appeared to her, we are told in Luke 1:26-33:

*"And in the sixth month the angel Gabriel was sent from God
unto a city of Galilee, named Nazareth, To a virgin espoused to a
man whose name was Joseph, of the house of David; and the
virgin's name was Mary. And the angel came in unto her, and
said, Hail, thou that art highly favoured, the Lord is with thee:
blessed art thou among women. And when she saw him, she was
troubled at his saying, and cast in her mind what manner of
salutation this should be. And the angel said unto her, Fear not,
Mary; for thou hast found favour with God. And, behold, thou
shalt conceive in thy womb, and bring forth a son, and shalt call
his name JESUS. He shall be great, and shall be called the Son
of the Highest: and the Lord God shall give unto him the throne
of his father David: And he shall reign over the house of Jacob for
ever; and of his kingdom there shall be no end."*

Was she a virgin when Jesus was born? Yes, she was, the Scripture here plainly says. Isaiah 7:14 had announced ahead of time,
"Behold, a virgin shall conceive, and bear a son, and shall call
his name Immanuel." The Hebrew word *almah* means "virgin";
it could mean nothing else. Only an unscholarly infidel would
deny that. I have searched carefully every time that word is used
in the Bible and it had to mean virgin. It was translated in the
Septuagint 200 years before Christ. There was no argument then,
and Jews did not know that Jesus would be the one they would

hate. So it was translated "virgin." The word used in everyday language meant that to them then in the Hebrew.

Then the King James translators put it "virgin," then the American Standard Version put it "virgin." More important, God, when He repeated the matter to Joseph in Matthew 1:23, put it, "Behold, a virgin shall be with child," and said it was the fulfillment of Isaiah 7:14. So we know that Mary was a virgin. It is also implied when God speaks of Jesus as the "only begotten Son," that is, the only Son physically begotten of God. It was taught also in Jeremiah when the Lord spoke of a great wonder that "a woman shall compass a man" (Jer. 31:22), not a man and a woman but a woman. It is implied also when God said to Eve that the Seed of the Woman should bruise the serpent's head and he should bruise His heel (Gen. 3:15). Evidently Mary, a dear virgin, miraculously was used to give birth to the Saviour.

And the Scripture says, "And the angel said unto her, Fear not, Mary: for thou hast found favour with God." Does that mean she had sought the favor of God? I think so. She gladly accepted by faith the great honor God gave her. It would mean some slander, some misunderstanding, when she was found to be with child, unmarried, but she faced whatever it cost to bear the Child, the Lord Jesus, the Son of God.

It is sweet to read how happy she was when she went to visit her cousin Elisabeth and they could rejoice together—Elisabeth, that she was to bear the son John the Baptist, and Mary who had just conceived the Lord Jesus.

Then Joseph had a dream. He had been troubled. In it he said, "How could Mary have fallen into sin? She is going to have a child!" How could he condemn her! He did not want her to be stoned as a harlot or as a fallen woman. He thought he would put her away privately, and that angel told him, "No, that which is conceived in her is of the Holy Ghost," and he was not to fear to take her as his wife. It was a fulfillment of prophecy. So Joseph took her as his wife, though he "knew her not" and the marriage was not consummated until after the Saviour was born, the Scripture tells us.

2. Mary Was a Good Woman but Not Supernatural

Our Catholic friends have made up a false teaching that Mary was conceived immaculately and was without the taint of inborn Adamic sin. That is wholly false and untrue to Scripture. No, when Mary met her cousin Elisabeth, she shouted out, filled with the Spirit of God and rejoicing, "My soul doth magnify the Lord, And my spirit hath rejoiced in God my Saviour" (Luke 1:46,47). A Saviour? Oh, then Mary was like I am, for I, too, am a sinner who had to have a Saviour. And, thank God, there is a Saviour for sinners like me and like Mary. Mary was an ordinary woman who put her trust in the Saviour and was saved.

There is also a foolish tradition that Mary was a perpetual virgin, that she was never really a wife to Joseph, that that so-called marriage was, in fact, a fraud and that Mary was a perpetual virgin. Nothing like that is taught in the Bible. When Jesus was born, the Bible calls Him "her firstborn son." She had other sons, and then daughters besides. Matthew 1:25 says Joseph, her husband, "knew her not till she had brought forth her firstborn son." And in Luke 2:7 it is said about Mary, "And she brought forth her firstborn son, and wrapped him in swaddling clothes. . . ." So Jesus was not the only child of Mary but only the firstborn.

Speaking in prophecy in Psalm 69:8, the Lord Jesus said, "I am become a stranger unto my brethren, and an alien unto my mother's children." The New Testament quotes the next verse as referring to Jesus; so this refers to Jesus, too.

Matthew 13:55 names His brothers—James, Joses, Simon and Judas. This "James the Lord's brother" Paul saw as he relates in Galatians 1:19. James wrote the book of James and the brother Jude wrote the book of Jude. But they were not converted until Christ died on the cross.

When Mary, the mother of Jesus, and his brothers came to see Him and could not get to Him for the press and someone told Him, "Thy mother and thy brethren stand without, desiring to see thee," Jesus answered and said unto them, "My mother and my brethren are these which hear the word of God, and do it" (Luke 8:20,21).

Evidently, then, any good woman who loves God and believes in Christ and does the will of God is as close to Christ as was His own mother spiritually. Oh, Mary was a good woman, but she was not sinless. She was greatly blessed in that she bore the Saviour, but that is all.

3. Mary Is Not Our "Mediatrix"; We Are Not to Pray to Her

Our Catholic friends ofter call her "Mother of God," but she is not that. She was the mother of the physical body of Jesus, but Jesus existed in the very beginning. He created the worlds. Catholics sometimes foolishly call her the "Mediatrix." So they give praise to Mary that ought to belong to Jesus Christ alone. "For there is one God, and one mediator between God and men, the man Christ Jesus; Who gave himself a ransom for all, to be testified in due time" (I Tim. 2:5,6).

I do not even know if Mary was a very good Christian in the sense of a developed, spiritually-minded, powerful Christian. Her other boys grew up unsaved, for in John 7:5 we are told about Jesus, "For neither did his brethren believe in him." So she had not won these boys. She knew who Jesus was and she had pondered in her heart the things revealed, and she knew that He was God's Son.

To say that Mary is the "Mediatrix," as Catholic leaders sometimes say, is blasphemy for it puts Mary in the place of Christ.

Once I preached in Washington, D.C., and at the close of the sermon a woman came to meet me and said, "I need to say two things to you. First, I must apologize. I felt it would not be right for me, a good Catholic, to go to other religious services that were not Catholic, but I thought, Well, the man has no robe. There are no candles. It is not really a religious service. But I was wrong. You had spoken but a few minutes when I knew that God was here and you were God's man! I hope you will forgive me. I didn't know."

I told her that she had not offended me and I was glad she could come. "And what is the other matter?" I asked.

She said, "You talked of people being born again. I know about

the Mass, and I know about confession and those things, but I do
not remember our priest ever telling us about being born again.
How do you get born again?"

How could I tell a good Catholic woman that priests at Masses
and confessions could not save? It would make her a poor
Catholic; it would not make her a Christian. So I said, "I will tell
you what we can do. I will ask you some Bible questions and that
will clear up the matter."

"Oh," she said in dismay, "no, I don't know anything about
the Bible. I know the prayer book pretty well, but I never read
the Bible much."

I assured her I would simply ask her to look at the Scripture
herself as I would show her and she could read the answer there.

I opened the Bible to I Timothy 2:5,6, "For there is one God,
and one mediator between God and men, the man Christ Jesus;
Who gave himself a ransom for all, to be testified in due time."

Now I asked, "How many gods are there?"

"Of course, there is just one," she replied.

But, with mock sternness, I said, "No; give it to me in the
words of the Bible!"

So she meekly said, "For there is one God. . . ."

"That is correct. Go to the head of the class. Now then, how
many mediators are there, how many go-betweens, how many in-
tercessors are there between God and men?" She knit her brows
and I said, "Read it from the Bible."

She read, "For there is one God, and one mediator between
God and men. . . ." She repeated it, "Just one."

Then I said, "Who is that one Mediator? Is it a preacher like
me?"

She shook her head.

I said, "Is it a priest?"

She said, "No."

I said, "Is it the virgin Mary?"

She looked up at me startled, and her eyes filled with tears.
With choked voice she said, "No, it is not the blessed virgin!"

Then I said, "Who is the one Mediator between God and men?
Read it!"

She read it. ". . .one mediator between God and men, the man Christ Jesus; Who gave himself a ransom for all, to be testified in due time." She was sobbing when she finished. Now she was ready to believe on the Lord Jesus Christ. Now she was ready to be saved. And she did call on the Lord and trust Him and was sweetly sure of her salvation. Then, as she dried her tears, she said, "I never would have believed that if you hadn't shown it to me in the Bible!"

Oh, the only Mediator between God and men is not Mary, but Jesus! He is our Mediator. Mary is not the "Mother of God." She was only the mother of the human body of Christ. Christ was in existence with the Father before the world began. She is not the "Queen of Heaven." She has no more authority or influence in Heaven than other women. She is not given any more prominence in the New Testament than other good Christian women.

But Mary was honored by getting to be the mother of the Lord Jesus.

We think Mary was probably not a very well-developed Christian. She did not win her younger sons to the Lord. They were not saved until Jesus came to the cross, as we understand from John 7:5. It is always wrong to pray to Mary or to worship Mary or give Mary special honor. To do so takes honor from Jesus Christ, who has all the right to it.

III. CHRIST AT NAZARETH

Nazareth is a great center of Christian attention because it was there the Lord Jesus lived most of His years on earth.

1. Nazareth Was the Home of Jesus for Twenty-Eight or Twenty-Nine Years

When Jesus was born in Bethlehem, the Wise Men from the East inquired at the palace of Herod at Jerusalem, "Where is he that is born King of the Jews? for we have seen his star in the east, and are come to worship him."

Herod inquired of Jewish leaders where. They said according to Old Testament prophecy the Messiah was to be born in Bethlehem as Micah 5:2 said. Herod planned to come and kill the Baby Jesus but God warned Joseph of it in a dream. So when King Herod had all the boy babies of Bethlehem killed up to two years old, Joseph and Mary and the Baby Jesus had already slipped away to Egypt. We suppose the gift of gold brought by the Wise Men supported them in these days when they fled into Egypt.

When Herod was dead (perhaps a year later), they returned to Galilee and went back to the old home town of Nazareth. And there Jesus grew up. And there He lived until He was about thirty years old. John the Baptist began his great ministry and was preaching down by Jordan and Jesus was baptized there and began His public ministry.

These years at Nazareth are mainly silent years. Jesus had not begun His ministry. He did no miracles. Yet we know that more than any other city in all Palestine, Nazareth saw much of the Lord Jesus.

He lived with Joseph and Mary. Since Joseph is not mentioned

An artist pictures the Holy Family

after Jesus was twelve, in Luke, chapter 2, we suppose that he died while Jesus was still in His teens. Jesus acted as head of the house then. When He moved to Capernaum, He took the family with Him. We suppose that He worked as a carpenter with Joseph and, perhaps, alone after Joseph died. He was perfect and sinless and blameless. He probably learned to cook since, after His resurrection, He broiled fish over a campfire for the apostles in John 21. He was familiar with all the manner of farms and husbandry and had the respect of all the people as a godly, trustworthy young Man.

2. "And Jesus Increased in Wisdom and Stature, and in Favour With God and Man"

It is a wonderful story in Luke, chapter 2, how Jesus went up to Jerusalem with Mary and Joseph. And when they started that long trek back to Galilee, there was no fret about Jesus. He was always trustworthy. Doubtless He was with some other friends in the caravan. But that night Jesus was not there. They went back to Jerusalem and found Him sitting in the Temple asking questions and giving answers to the scribes and teachers. They were astonished. When His mother told Him they had "sought thee sorrowing," He said, "Wist ye not that I must be about my Father's business?" He was gently rebuking her. Joseph was not His father. He must be learning all He could now before He began His public ministry.

It is strange that "Jesus increased in wisdom and stature, and in favour with God and man" (Luke 2:52). How could Jesus, the sinless, perfect God in human form, grow in wisdom? I think we can understand that the Lord Jesus gladly laid aside much of the outward show of His deity and much of the wisdom and knowledge which He had from before the beginning of the world. He chose to be a Man, with man's temptations and trials, but not with man's sin. So He "took on him the form of a servant." He emptied Himself somewhat of the outward manifestations of deity. He set out to learn as other boys must learn. He grew in body as other boys grow.

The Scripture tells us that He "learned obedience by the things which he suffered" (Heb. 5:8). So the Lord Jesus learned hard work and temptations and entered into the experiences that others had. If He is to be our Saviour, He must be like us in all the things that are possible except in the matter of sin.

He grew "in favour with God." That is strange, too, isn't it? But God the Father loved His Son because He offered Himself as a Sacrifice, and if righteousness brings approval of God, then the Father is more and more pleased with His Son. So Jesus grew to manhood being subject to His mother and His foster father Joseph. And all the mothers would say to the boys around there, "You ought to be like Jesus. Don't you see how good He is?"

We may be sure that Jesus studied the Scriptures earnestly. When He came back to Nazareth He attended the synagogue "as he was wont." They asked Him to read because they knew how well He knew the Bible. He was the best Reader and the best One to explain the Scriptures. So they gave Him the roll of Isaiah and "He found the place where it is written, The Spirit of the Lord is upon me. . ." (Luke 4:16,17,18). He knew where it was and turned to it. Jesus knew the Scriptures and loved them. All of His life on earth would be spent beautifully and carefully fulfilling the Scriptures.

When Jesus came to John to be baptized of him, John hesitated. John did not know that Jesus was the Messiah until He was baptized and the Holy Spirit came visibly upon Him in the form like a dove. But already He knew that Jesus was so good and pure and clean, and John had a holy reverence for Him. He said, "I have need to be baptized of thee, and comest thou to me?" You can see that though people did not know He was the Messiah (except, perhaps, His mother Mary), yet the good people who knew Him knew Him to be holy and good.

3. Jesus Returned to Nazareth After He Began His Public Ministry

When Jesus was baptized by John in the River Jordan there appeared upon Him the Holy Spirit in a form like a dove, and John knew this was the Messiah. Then the Holy Spirit was upon Him in mighty power. He was led into the wilderness to be tempted, for if He is to be my Saviour, He must know all the temptations and must have had victory where I have had failure.

Then He began to preach the Gospel. Up to this time He had never preached a sermon, never healed a sick body, never touched a blind eye, never won a soul. Now He is anointed to preach. So back He goes to Nazareth where He was brought up. There He went into the synagogue, as He had done for so many years when He lived there, and they gave Him the book of Isaiah to read. He read Isaiah 61:1, "The Spirit of the Lord is upon me, because he hath anointed me to preach the gospel to the poor; he hath sent me to heal the brokenhearted, to preach deliverance to the captives, and recovering of sight to the blind, to set at liberty them that are bruised, To preach the acceptable year of the Lord" (Luke 4:18,19). They marvelled: "Is this the same Jesus?" There was a power about Him they had not seen before. So Jesus read that Scripture and said, "This day is this scripture fulfilled in your ears." Oh, the mighty change when one comes out in the power of God, as Jesus then did!

Ah, but He had before this worked His first miracle in Cana of Galilee. He had healed others in Capernaum. Now they wanted Him to work miracles there. But Jesus knew that "a prophet is not without honour, but in his own country, and among his own kin, and in his own house" (Mark 6:4). So they could not immediately believe that this was the Messiah, the Saviour. Why, they had known Him for these near thirty years!

And when He did not perform many mighty works there because of their unbelief, they hated Him and rushed Him out of town to the "Hill of Precipitation." There they would have hurled Him down from the mount on which the city was built, but He slipped away from them. There in Nazareth He could do no mighty works because of their unbelief, the Scripture says.

Is not Nazareth then a wonderful expression of how the Lord Jesus came to earth to live among us and die for sinners? It was in a little known province. It was a small city. Jesus lived among common people. He worked at a carpenter's trade with His foster father. He lived some thirty years before He set out in His public ministry as a Saviour because, first of all, He must be God's pattern man, God's perfect man, the Second Adam. As Adam led the whole race into sin when he sinned and there was a taint on his bloodline, so the Lord Jesus died for the sins of the whole world and, "As in Adam all die, even so in Christ shall all be made alive" (I Cor. 15:22). That is, Jesus died for the sins of the whole world, and whatever taint of Adam's sin is in a child, that does not damn him. His own personal sin makes him a lost sinner when he comes to know right from wrong.

But Jesus was ". . .in all points tempted like as we are, yet without sin" (Heb. 4:15). Jesus was a Friend of sinners and walked among them for many years. The Lord Jesus knew the frailties of man and needed not that any man should tell Him.

O Nazareth, with common streets and walks and houses and common people, the Lord Jesus lived among you there! He saw the streets, too, with donkeys carrying loads, and women carrying their pitchers of water from the well, and men working in the fields or bargaining in the stores.

So Jesus can live in my house and live in your house. He can walk my streets with me. He can sit at my table while I eat. He is so close He can hear me when I pray. He cares about everything that happens to me.

O Nazareth, commonplace Nazareth, Nazareth of the common people, Nazareth of poor, sinful, dying people, you are a type of this whole world for which Jesus died! I am so glad Jesus came to live as a Boy and a Man so He can make a perfect example, and where I failed, He did not fail. He is fit to be my Substitute, my Saviour.

VI. At Capernaum Where Jesus Did Most of His Mighty Works: Woe, Capernaum!

"And thou, Capernaum, which art exalted unto heaven, shalt be brought down to hell: for if the mighty works, which have been done in thee, had been done in Sodom, it would have remained until this day. But I say unto you, That it shall be more tolerable for the land of Sodom in the day of judgment, than for thee."—Matt. 11:23,24.

After Jesus was baptized and filled with the Spirit and then went into the wilderness for forty days of great temptation, He moved from Galilee to Capernaum and made that His home during the rest of His ministry. He preached throughout that area and went to Jerusalem on feast days and eventually was tried and crucified. But most of His earthly ministry was in and around Capernaum. Capernaum was on the northwest shore of the little Sea of Galilee, fifteen miles long and seven and one half miles wide.

In the time of Christ the area around Galilee was more thickly settled than today. We believe that the rainfall was more and the ground more productive. Capernaum was once on the principal roads from the Fertile Crescent around and down through Galilee and the Valley of Megiddon to the country of the Philistines and on into Egypt.

Now, there are the remains of a synagogue built in the second or third century. It appears that this synagogue was built on the site of the one which Jesus attended and where Jesus preached often in Capernaum.

The Catholic Order of Franciscan Friars who keep the place now have decided they have discovered the remains of Peter's house and they want to make that a shrine in the familiar way that the Catholics manufacture tradition and relics. Of course, the simple truth is that Peter did not live in Capernaum but at Bethsaida near by as John 1:44 says, "the city of Andrew and Peter." Here I have come fourteen times; I know that on the shore here nearby Jesus walked and here He called Peter, Andrew, James and John to follow Him by the seaside and at the market place He called Levi, or Matthew, who was a tax collector. Here at Capernaum and nearby were the most of the mighty works of Jesus done in His earthly ministry. And as I stood and taught my people and preached a bit, standing on the stone floor of that ancient synagogue, I thought maybe Jesus stood in the same place or sat on the same stone bench on the side. Oh, Capernaum, how greatly you were blessed!

I. HOW MANY MIGHTY WORKS OF JESUS WERE DONE AT CAPERNAUM!

We say "mighty works" because that is what the Bible calls the works of Jesus at Capernaum and near there.

In Matthew 11:20 we are told, "Then began he to upbraid the cities wherein most of his mighty works were done, because they repented not."

When Jesus returned for a short time to Nazareth nearby, ". . . he taught them in their synagogue, insomuch that they were astonished, and said, Whence hath this man this wisdom, and these mighty works?" (Matt. 13:54). Herod, the tetrarch of Galilee, heard of the fame of Jesus "and said unto his servants, This is John the Baptist; he is risen from the dead; and therefore mighty works do shew forth themselves in him" (Matt. 14:3). Herod was mistaken; it was not John the Baptist, for John the Baptist did no mighty works like these. Mark 6:14 also records the words of Herod that ". . . mighty works do shew forth themselves in him."

Immediately after His baptism and testing He had gone to Nazareth and preached in the synagogue with mighty power and told them how the Scripture, Isaiah 61:1, was now fulfilled in Him:

"The Spirit of the Lord is upon me, because he hath anointed me to preach the gospel to the poor; he hath sent me to heal the brokenhearted, to preach deliverance to the captives, and recovering of sight to the blind, to set at liberty them that are bruised . . . And all bare him witness, and wondered at the gracious words which proceeded out of his mouth. And they said, Is not this Joseph's son?"—Luke 4:18,22.

And because He did not do there at Nazareth some of the great works they heard had been done in Capernaum, they rose up in wrath and rushed Him out of the city and tried to cast Him down from the "Hill of Precipitation"! Ah, there were mighty works that Jesus did there!

1. How Seriously God Wants Us to Remember, to Emphasize, to Marvel at His Mighty Works

Divine inspiration insists that the works of Jesus were "mighty works." Well, God calls us to consider, "The heavens declare the glory of God; and the firmament sheweth his handywork. Day unto day uttereth speech, and night unto night sheweth knowledge. There is no speech nor language, where their voice is not heard" (Ps. 19:1-3). God intends nature to preach to us always about a mighty God who made and controls all things.

In Romans 1:18-20, God tells us:

"For the wrath of God is revealed from heaven against all ungodliness and unrighteousness of men, who hold the truth in unrighteousness; Because that which may be known of God is manifest in them; for God hath shewed it unto them. For the invisible things of him from the creation of the world are clearly seen, being understood by the things that are made, even his eternal power and Godhead; so that they are without excuse."

One who sees God's creation and continues in unrighteousness has the wrath of God upon him! And they are without excuse "because that which may be known of God is manifest in them; for God hath shewed it unto them." The invisible things of creation witness of God, and there is something wicked about a man who is not moved by the awesome fact of such a mighty God.

That chapter continues to tell us how, after the flood, so many people turned their hearts away from God and God turned them over to a reprobate mind. So intelligent, cultivated, civilized people turned into tribes of heathens and savages and idol worshipers and sex perverts because they did not want to retain God in their knowledge! God wants man to be impressed and to marvel and to remember His mighty works.

So when God brought the children out of Egypt, with what signs and wonders it was! How He turned the waters of the river into blood, brought the plague of frogs, of lice, of locusts, of midnight darkness, even the death of the firstborn. How marvelously God opened the Red Sea and brought them safely through; how He slew the hosts of the Egyptians behind them; how He led them by a cloudy pillar; how He fed them manna from Heaven; how He cared for them forty years in the wilderness!

Oh, the Lord said to them again and again, "Do not forget"! They were to have the passover supper every year and were to tell their children the story of the death of the firstborn in Egypt and how the death angel had passed over every house that had the blood of the lamb on the doorpost. They were annually to have the feast of tabernacles, and they were to make them booths from branches to remind themselves of the forty years in the wilderness that God cared for His people in a desert country, with no cities, no fields, and no human resources. And when God gave them the Ten Commandments, He started out saying, "I am the Lord thy God, which have brought thee out of the land of Egypt, out of the house of bondage" (Exod. 20:1).

Who is there who can look at the starry heavens and not know that there is a mighty God! The song, "How Great Thou Art!" says:

> O Lord my God! When I in awesome wonder
>   Consider all the worlds Thy hands have made,
> I see the stars, I hear the rolling thunder,
>   Thy pow'r through out the universe displayed,
> Then sings my soul, my Saviour God to Thee;
>   How great Thou art, how great Thou art!

Then sings my soul, my Saviour God to Thee;
How great Thou art, how great Thou art!

Oh, then, surely the people of all the area around Capernaum where Jesus did His most marvelous works must be held greatly to account for the way they listen or do not listen, the way they obey or do not obey, the way they love the Lord Jesus or hate Him.

2. Consider the Wonders of Christ's Ministry Here About Capernaum

The first thing Jesus did when He came to Capernaum was to cast out demons. "And they were astonished at his doctrine: for his word was with power" (Luke 4:32). In that synagogue was a man with the "spirit of an unclean devil" and the devil cried out that Christ should let them alone, that they knew Him. They admitted He was the Holy One of God. But Jesus commanded the demon to hold his peace and come out. The devil threw the man in the midst and came out of him. "And they were all amazed, and spake among themselves, saying, What word is this! for with authority and power he commandeth the unclean spirits, and they come out. And the fame of him went out into every place of the country round about" (Luke 4:31-37).

3. Then Jesus Immediately Went to the Home of Peter and Raised Peter's Wife's Mother From the Sickbed

She had "a great fever." Christ rebuked the fever. "Immediately she arose and ministered unto them" (Luke 4:38,39). In the evening many brought those who were possessed of devils and with unclean spirits that He should cast them out and He did.

4. He Healed a Leper at His Simple Request

Nearby Capernaum in a certain city, when a poor leper came and fell on his face before Jesus saying, "Lord, if thou wilt, thou canst make me clean," with a tender hand, Jesus touched him and said, "I will: be thou clean. And immediately the leprosy departed from him" (Luke 5:12,13). How famous Jesus became!

5. Then Jesus Stopped to Forgive a Sinner and Heal a Palsied Man

It was in a home where Jesus was preaching that the house and yard was filled with people. The poor people brought a poor, palsied man who longed to be saved and wanted to get to Jesus. Since they could not get in the door, they went on top of the house and tore up the tile roof and let the sick man down before Jesus and "when he saw their faith, he said unto him, Man, thy sins are forgiven thee." When the Pharisees argued, "Who can forgive sins, but God alone?" the Lord Jesus then healed the man and told him to take up his bed and go home to his house.

6. On the Sabbath, a Man With a Withered Hand Was Healed

Another Sabbath day in the synagogue there came a man whose right hand was withered. How the critical scribes and Pharisees watched Jesus, hoping to accuse Him if He healed one on the Sabbath day! But He had the man stand up in the midst and stretch forth his hand, "and his hand was restored whole as the other." Ah, He knew their thoughts, yet His compassion continued to heal (Luke 6:6-11).

7. The Centurion's Servant Healed

A centurion had a dear servant who was sick. He felt himself not worthy to have Jesus come to his house, but said, "Lord, trouble not thyself: for I am not worthy that thou shouldest enter under my roof: Wherefore neither thought I myself worthy to come unto thee: but say in a word, and my servant shall be healed." Oh, he said, "When I speak to a soldier, he goes or to a servant, come, do this, he does it." So he trusted the Lord. How gladly Jesus healed that centurion's servant and praised his great faith (Luke 7:1-10).

8. A Widow's Son Raised From the Dead

At Nain, nearby, Jesus preached and as He went into a city, coming out of the city is a sad procession. It is a funeral! The young man whose body was borne on the litter was the only son of a widow and Jesus had compassion and said to her, "Weep

not. And he came and touched the bier: and they that bare him
stood still. And he said, Young man, I say unto thee, Arise. And
he that was dead sat up, and began to speak. And he delivered
Him to his mother. And there came a fear on all" (Luke 7:13-16).
Oh, there were mighty works that Jesus did!

9. Many Other Marvels Did Jesus Near or at Capernaum

John the Baptist sent his messengers and they saw many
mighty works! Oh, Jesus stopped the storm on the Sea of Galilee
at a word. He cast out the demons of the man of Gadara, a wild
man who had everybody in terror, a man who could not be bound
with chains and sent him out to witness. A woman who came
behind Him touched His garment and was healed of her issue of
blood in a moment. Jairus' daughter was raised from the dead.
Then Jesus fed the five thousand men beside women and
children with five little barley loaves and two small fishes! That
was a miracle of creation as literal and real as when Jesus
Himself created the worlds in the beginning. Then He fed the
four thousand.

What marvels Jesus did in and around Capernaum!

Fear fell on many. Many rejected Him and hated Him. But
men must give an account when they come to see or hear such
mighty things done by the Son of God.

II. HERE AT CAPERNAUM AND ABOUT, JESUS CALLED HIS DISCIPLES

It was from the province of Galilee in and around Capernaum
where Jesus called the twelve disciples. At Pentecost people
would remark about these twelve disciples, "Behold, are not all
these which speak Galilaeans? And how hear we every man in
our own tongue, wherein we were born?" (Acts 2:7,8). Those at
the house of the high priest when Jesus was tried and condemned
identified Peter as one of His disciples, saying, "Of a truth this
fellow also was with him: for he is a Galilaean" (Luke 22:59).

1. Here Jesus, in a Dramatic Way, Calls Peter and Andrew, James and John, to Follow Him

That wonderful story is told in Luke 5:1-11.

The words of Jesus to Peter and Andrew are given in Matthew 4:19: "And he saith unto them, Follow me, and I will make you fishers of men." And the same invitation is repeated in Mark 1:17, "Come ye after me, and I will make you to become fishers of men." Yes, "And straightway they forsook their nets, and followed him" (Mark 1:18).

Below: author and Dr. Bill Rice

Our boat arrives at Capernaum on Galilee.

What a picture Jesus gave here in this miracle! Peter and Andrew had fished all night and caught nothing. Now they washed their nets in disappointment and waited for another night to fish again. But after Jesus had sat in their boat and preached and said, "Launch out into the deep, and let down your nets for a draught," they had little faith—they let down one net. But it was instantly filled and they had to call for their partners, James and John, to come help them, and they gathered in two boatloads of fish! No wonder Peter was astonished. No wonder he felt unfit to even be in the presence of such a mighty Miracle-Worker, God in human form. But Jesus assured him, "Henceforth thou shalt catch men."

I think that net full of fish must have prefigured the mighty reaping of souls at Pentecost and beyond. That lesson was enough for Peter and Andrew and also for James and John. We are told that Jesus went to James and John and called them and "they immediately left the ship and their father, and followed him" (Matt. 4:22).

2. It Was at Capernaum Also That He Called Matthew the Publican

Matthew was a tax collector. His other name is Levi. He was sitting "at the receipt of custom" at Capernaum and Jesus passed by and simply said unto him, "Follow me. And he arose, and followed him" (Matt. 9:9). Oh, how glad the man was to give up a good job and the sure income from the government, to now follow Jesus and preach the Gospel! He had been a very worldly man, of course, working with the Romans and the publicans who were often despised and usually crooked. Now, Matthew called together all his old buddies—the publicans and sinners—for a great supper at his house. I suppose he had a large home, and other tax collectors and the "sinners" would have been those not morally clean, drunkards and harlots and such. They came, and Jesus was invited to the house to speak to these sinners. What a wonderful opportunity it was!

I remember when a dear couple in Miami, Florida, urged me to come and preach to a family reunion they had in a park on the 4th of July which was also their wedding anniversary. At Vickery, Texas, I was invited to speak at a football banquet. The football team had made good; now they were to be honored at a banquet. The teachers, the coach, the sweethearts of the team, their dads and mothers, etc., were invited. I preached to them after the dinner. Three of the team were already Christians. The other eight first-string members were converted that night, because we made an occasion of such a dinner as Levi had.

But the Pharisees and scribes were indignant. They came to the disciples saying:

"Why eateth your Master with publicans and sinners? But when Jesus heard that, he said unto them, They that be whole

need not a physician, but they that are sick. But go ye and learn what that meaneth, I will have mercy, and not sacrifice: for I am not come to call the righteous, but sinners to repentance."— Matt. 9:11-13.

Oh, how glad Jesus was to preach the Gospel to sinners! He never had a sinner lead in prayer, nor to be chairman of His campaign. He never called such a sinner a Christian. He did call them to become Christians.

That was an old, old complaint they had against Jesus, and Jesus gave the three parables in Luke 15 to illustrate that, after "the Pharisees and scribes murmured, saying, This man receiveth sinners, and eateth with them."

We do not know the details of just when each one of the others were particularly told they were to be disciples. After His baptism in the River Jordan,

"The day following Jesus would go forth into Galilee, and findeth Philip, and saith unto him, Follow me. Now Philip was of Bethsaida, the city of Andrew and Peter, Philip findeth Nathanael, and saith unto him, We have found him, of whom Moses in the law, and the prophets, did write, Jesus of Nazareth, the son of Joseph."—John 1:43-45.

So, in one way or another, all the twelve disciples were saved and recruited and committed to be disciples and witnesses for Jesus, and all were from Galilee, in the area in and near Capernaum.

3. The Call for All Is for Soul Winning

It was a dramatic time, when the Lord Jesus had Peter and Andrew launch out into the deep and let down a net and suddenly the net was full to breaking and they had to call for their partners James and John and their father Zebedee to help them bring in the two boatloads of fish. I do not wonder that Peter was overwhelmed, conscious of sin and weakness in the face of such a miracle. And Jesus said to Simon, "Fear not; from henceforth thou shalt catch men" (Luke 5:10).

The call was to catch men, to get people saved! So Jesus said to all of them in Matthew 4:19, "Follow me, and I will make you fishers of men." Again the call is stated in Mark 1:17, "Come ye after me, and I will make you to become fishers of men." He did not say to one, "I will call you to be a Bible teacher," and to another, "I call you to be a teacher," and to another, "I call you to be an administrator or an educator." All these things may be involved incidentally, but the call is always to the one main thing—come and get people saved. "From henceforth thou shalt catch men."

This preacher is an editor as well as an evangelist, and I know the burden God has laid on me to make a climate for soul winning, to train people to win souls, to stir the hearts of pastors to grow great soul-winning churches. But that does not excuse me from the one direct call that God has for everybody—"henceforth thou shalt catch men."

Should not every Christian be concerned with the one thing dearest to the heart of Jesus Christ, dearest to the heart of God? That, obviously, is soul winning. That is what Jesus came into the world for. First Timothy 1:15 says, "This is a faithful saying, and worthy of all acceptation, that Christ Jesus came into the world to save sinners; of whom I am chief." He came to save sinners. There are a thousand other good things, results of Christianity, but the one great consideration is this: Jesus came to save sinners, He died to keep people out of Hell. There is nothing as important in the plan of God as getting people saved.

And remember the Great Commission. Not an incidental instruction, but the GREAT COMMISSION. It is the main command Jesus gave, the all-inclusive command He repeated five times in the forty days after His resurrection as stated in Mark 16:15, "Go ye into all the world, and preach the gospel to every creature." Not to every congregation, but to every creature. And the preaching is not the homiletic message of the pulpit necessarily, but the earnest witness of a Christian, whether lay Christian or preacher.

And as the Great Commission puts it in Matthew 28:19,20, "Go ye therefore, and teach all nations, baptizing them in the name of the Father, and of the Son, and of the Holy Ghost: Teaching them to observe all things whatsoever I have commanded you." The great plan is to get people saved and when we get people saved, then they are to be baptized, to be branded, to be lined up and committed. And then they are to be taught to *do just what the apostles did.* Not simply taught doctrine, not simply taught Scripture, not simply taught prophecy; they are to be taught to do what Jesus Christ told the apostles and all of us to do, that is, to get people saved, to get them baptized and to teach them to win souls, too.

That, I say, is the Great Commission. No other command of Jesus compares with that in all-inclusive importance for every Christian. Everybody who is saved ought to be taught to win souls.

That is the way this last sweet promise in the New Testament commands us, also. The Lord Jesus, closing the canon of Scripture, said, "The Spirit and the bride say, Come. And let him that heareth say, Come. And let him that is athirst come. And whosoever will, let him take the water of life freely" (Rev. 22:17). So the Scripture says that as the Holy Spirit calls and as the heavenly bride, let's say, prepared as a bride adorned for her husband, calls, so every Christian who has heard it should tell it. "Let him that heareth say, Come."

I am saying that every call of God is a call to soul winning. In Luke 14 is the parable of the man who made a great supper and bade many, "And sent *his servant* at supper time to say to them that were bidden, Come. . . ." The only servant that man had was out knocking on doors to get a crowd for the supper.

In the parable in Matthew 22 the king had a wedding for his son and sent *his servants* at suppertime to call people to the supper. All the servants the king had were getting people ready for the supper. Surely we must remember that the call of Jesus for the disciples at Capernaum and His call for Christians now is to win souls. Every Christian ought to be a soul winner.

But does not Ephesians 4:11 say, "And he gave some, apostles; and some, prophets; and some evangelists; and some, pastors and teachers"? Oh, yes, it does. And all of these—apostles, prophets, evangelists, pastors, teachers—all "for the work of the ministry" and ". . . by that which every joint supplieth, according to the effectual working in the measure of every part, *maketh increase of the body* unto the edifying of itself in love." Everyone God calls is to 'make increase of the body,' that is, get people ready for that grand assembly at the rapture when we are to be called out to meet Christ. I am saying that the call of Christ for disciples is a call to win souls.

III. THE CURSE ON THE FAVORED CITIES

We hear liberals speak of the meek and lowly Jesus, that God is a God of love. They do not want any preaching of divine judgment and of Hell and the certain punishment that comes from sin. Ah, but the cities where Jesus did His mighty work were put under a curse for not receiving Him and believing on Him.

1. Woe Pronounced on Capernaum, Chorazin, Bethsaida

In Matthew 11:20-24, we hear the strong and solemn judgment of Jesus on these cities.

"Then began he to upbraid the cities wherein most of his mighty works were done, because they repented not: Woe unto thee, Chorazin! woe unto thee, Bethsaida! for if the mighty works, which were done in you, had been done in Tyre and Sidon, they would have repented long ago in sackcloth and ashes. But I say unto you, It shall be more tolerable for Tyre and Sidon at the day of judgment, than for you. And thou, Capernaum, which art exalted unto heaven, shalt be brought down to hell: for if the mighty works which have been done in thee, had been done in Sodom, it would have remained until this day. But I say unto you, That it shall be more tolerable for the land of Sodom in the day of judgment, than for thee."

Notice that this judgment is because they repented not when the mighty works of Jesus were done in their midst. Jesus says plainly that if those mighty works had been done in Tyre and Sidon, they would have repented long ago in sackcloth and ashes. He said that the people of Capernaum would find that it would be more tolerable for those of Sodom in the day of judgment than for those in Capernaum where Jesus had preached in their streets and in their houses, attended their synagogue,

Ruins of Synagogue at Capernaum

healed the sick and blind, the leper and the palsied, and cast out devils there.

I have gone many times to what is now known as the ruins of Capernaum. The place was long unknown. At last they have excavated what seems clearly to be the remains of a synagogue at Capernaum. The floor, the foundation, is there and some restored pillars and part of a wall. There are tremendous carved columns and capitals and figures about, and that is all that now remains of the city of Capernaum.

That synagogue where Jesus preached so often was destroyed and this, we think, is the ruins of one built again, perhaps on the same grounds in the second or third century. But Capernaum was utterly destroyed. It is no more a city.

What about Chorazin and Bethsaida? We do not even know for sure where they were. On the map in the back of my Bible there are two places named for Chorazin and Bethsaida but in each case there is a question mark by the name, for the map makers do not know and nobody else knows for sure where these cities were. We think they were close to Capernaum. There people heard Jesus and saw His mighty works and now with the woe of

God upon them, these cities have passed out of existence and those people who heard the Gospel and saw the works of Jesus went to judgment, too. They did not repent.

Tiberias is still there on the western shore of the little Sea of Galilee. And so is Nazareth, and so Nain, where the widow's son was raised from the dead, and Cana, where Jesus made the water into wine. Jericho is still a city. But Capernaum, Chorazin and Bethsaida long ago passed out of existence.

2. God Has Brought Such a Curse on Many Cities

God destroyed the mighty city of Babylon because of her sins. He says:

"Behold, I will stir up the Medes against them, which shall not regard silver; and as for gold, they shall not delight in it. Their bows also shall dash the young men to pieces; and they shall have no pity on the fruit of the womb; their eye shall not spare children. And Babylon, the glory of kingdoms, the beauty of the Chaldees' excellency, shall be as when God overthrew Sodom and Gomorrah. It shall never be inhabited, neither shall it be dwelt in from generation to generation: neither shall the Arabian pitch tent there; neither shall the shepherds make their fold there. But wild beasts of the desert shall lie there; and their houses shall be full of doleful creatures; and owls shall dwell there, and satyrs shall dance there. And wild beasts of the islands shall cry in their desolate houses, and dragons in their pleasant palaces: and her time is near to come, and her days shall not be prolonged."—Isa. 13:17-22.

There is a town called Babylon, but it is not the same Babylon of Bible times. The ruins of that giant city are witness to the curse of God on those who go on unrepentant in their sins.

Tyre was another city that was judged because of its sins. Ezekiel 26:3-5 tells us:

"Therefore thus saith the Lord God; Behold, I am against thee, O Tyrus, and will cause many nations to come up against thee, as the sea causeth his waves to come up. And they shall destroy the walls of Tyrus, and break down her towers: I will also scrape her dust from her, and make her like the top of a rock. It

shall be a place for the spreading of nets in the midst of the sea: for I have spoken it, saith the Lord God: and it shall become a spoil to the nations."

So, against Tyre came Nebuchadnezzar with his great armies to "slay with the sword the daughters in the field: and he shall make a fort against thee, and cast a mount against thee, and lift up the buckler against thee. And he shall set engines of war against thy walls, and with his axes he shall break down thy towers" (Ezek. 26:8,9). Then later, Alexander the Great would come against that city, and when it moved from its site on the shore out to an island, then they scraped the dust down to bare rock to make a causeway out to the island to take the city. Ah, so judgment comes on the city that goes on in sin.

So it was with Sodom and Gomorrah, Admah and Zeboim, as we learn in Genesis 19:24,25 and Deuteronomy 29:23. He poured out fire and brimstone from the Lord out of Heaven and destroyed those cities. Now the ruins are covered in the lower part of the Dead Sea as the waters have been slowly rising through the centuries.

3. We Know the Awful Judgment on Israel Because of Their Sins

Before the Babylonian captivity the wickedness and idolatry of the people increased and bloodshed abounded so that there was no remedy but captivity. So, with an awful destruction, first the Northern Kingdom was carried away (II Kings 17:6), then in Judah Jerusalem was destroyed, the Temple torn down, the walls broken up and the choicest of all Israel were taken in captivity.

Again after Christ came and preached so wonderfully in Jerusalem, He told them, "And when ye shall see Jerusalem compassed with armies, then know that the desolation thereof is nigh" (Luke 21:20). He told His disciples, ". . . There shall not be left here one stone upon another, that shall not be thrown down" (Matt. 24:2). He wept over Jerusalem and its coming doom and said, "Behold, your house is left unto you desolate" (Luke 13:35).

So Jews were scattered to all the world and are today, still under the curse of a people who do not turn to Christ and serve Him.

What about our country where about a million unborn babies were killed "legally" last year by wicked women who just wanted the pleasures of a wife or mistress but not the responsibilities of a mother, and by the wicked doctors who were glad to take money to murder? And when it is legalized by law and recommended by Baptist conventions, what hope is there that America can escape the judgment of God? Will it be war as has sometimes been in the past? Will it be revolution? Will it be financial disaster and utter depression? I do not know, but I know that no city nor nation can get by with sin.

Let the destruction that came to Capernaum, and which came to Sodom and Gomorrah, Admah and Zeboim and other cities, warn everybody that where Christ has done mighty works, people will be held accountable for it.

Jesus told His disciples in Matthew 10:14, "And whosoever shall not receive you, nor hear your words, when ye depart out of that house or city, shake off the dust of your feet."

Early in 1936 I had a citywide campaign in Binghamton, New York, in the Binghamton Theater, seating 1,700. Although we had great crowds and many, many people saved, the Pastor's Conference, principally liberal, unbelieving men, scoffed publicly and in the newspapers about the revival. When I likened Binghamton to Sodom and Gomorrah, they were shocked, saying that Binghamton was the Athens of New York State. The police department wired back to Dallas to find if there were any criminal charges against this preacher!

Before I drove out of the city, after five weeks, I stood out on the snow, shook the dust off my feet and asked God to hold the city accountable for the preaching they had heard and the great number of conversions they had seen. Within a day a great thaw came and the nineteen inches of accumulated snow up and down that valley melted and a great flood inundated much of the city. There were millions of dollars of damage, and some deaths.

O Capernaum! How you ought to have listened to the dear

Saviour! How you ought to have marveled at the mighty works He did there! How you ought to have repented of your sins!

So ought everyone who reads these words. God has been so good. You must give an account. Turn today from sin in humble penitence.

VII. The Temple in Jerusalem
With Jesus

"That the Lord appeared to Solomon the second time, as he had appeared unto him at Gibeon. And the Lord said unto him, I have heard thy prayer and thy supplication, that thou hast made before me: I have hallowed this house, which thou hast built, to put my name there for ever; and mine eyes and mine heart shall be there perpetually."—I Kings 9:2,3.

When we drove around the Mount of Olives, coming up from Jericho and my eyes fell for the first time upon the city of Jerusalem, how my heart burned within me! There across the small vale of Cedron was the wall of the city, the never-opened Eastern Gate, and the site of Solomon's Temple and of the Temple in Jesus' day. It occupies the southeast corner of the walled city, a great raised platform. On it are two Moslem mosques: the Dome of the Rock, one of the most beautiful buildings in the world, octagonal with a golden dome; and the Mosque el Aksa.

Of course, Solomon's Temple was destroyed by Nebuchadnezzar at the time of the Babylonian captivity. Then Ezra built there a Temple on his return after seventy years. Then Herod the Great built a beautiful Temple (forty-six years in building), a little before Christ appeared there. That Temple was destroyed in the destruction of Jerusalem by Titus and his Roman army in A.D. 70. Then the platform was rebuilt by the Crusaders and the wall around Jerusalem was rebuilt by Suleiman the Magnificent. But the area is authentically the site of Solomon's Temple.

Jerusalem from the air, with Dome of the Rock at center

Underneath are great arched caverns which are sometimes called Solomon's Stables but are really stables of the Crusaders. Underneath also are cisterns which collect water.

From this platform, the site of the ancient Temple, one may climb stone stairs to the city wall and walk along the top behind a bulwark with loop holes and slits built for the protection of those who might defend the city against an army.

Since God promised Solomon, "I have hallowed this house, which thou hast built, to put my name there for ever; and mine eyes and mine heart shall be there perpetually," we judge this place is dear to God as it is dear to millions of people.

I. THIS IS ON THE END OF MOUNT MORIAH WHERE ABRAHAM WOULD HAVE OFFERED ISAAC

Yes, the place where Abraham was to offer Isaac, the threshing floor of Araunah the Jebusite which David purchased for sacrifices and Moriah where the Temple was built, are the same place.

1. God Sent Abraham From Beer-Sheba to Moriah for This Proposed Sacrifice

In Genesis 22:1,2 God tested Abraham:

"And it came to pass after these things, that God did tempt Abraham, and said unto him, Abraham: and he said, Behold, here I am. And he said, Take now thy son, thine only son Isaac, whom thou lovest, and get thee into the land of Moriah; and offer him there for a burnt-offering upon one of the mountains which I will tell thee of."

So Abraham got up early, saddled the donkey and took two of his young men with him and Isaac, chopped the wood for the burnt offering and took his journey. The third day he came to this place. The two servants with them were left at the foot of the hill, and Abraham took the wood and laid it upon the back of his son, and he took the fire in his hand, and a knife, and they went together. Then on the mountain Abraham made an altar and bound Isaac and laid him on that altar and raised the knife to kill him. Oh, we know the broken heart of Abraham, but he would honor God and trust that God would raise the lad again, we are told in Hebrews 11:17-19. But God stopped the hand with the knife and Abraham found a ram caught by the horns in the bushes.

When Isaac, so accustomed to sacrifices, had said, "Behold the fire and the wood: but where is the lamb for a burnt-offering?" Abraham said, "My son, God will provide himself a lamb for a burnt-offering" (Gen. 22:7,8). Now here is the lamb God has provided and so they sacrificed the ram and Abraham gladly took his son, who was given back to his bosom, back to Beersheba. But that place was dear to God's heart. He had selected it for a purpose.

2. David Purchased This Spot From Araunah the Jebusite for a Place of Sacrifice

In II Samuel 24 and in I Chronicles 21 we are told how David had been proud and vain about the great army God had given him. He wanted the people numbered. For his pride God sent a curse upon the people, and people were dying, but David was instructed to go to Araunah the Jebusite and rear an altar unto the Lord there. The Jebusites dwelt in Jerusalem.

David came to buy the place which Araunah would have gladly given to him, along with oxen for the sacrifice and the threshing instruments for wood, but David would not take it free. He said:

"Nay; but I will surely buy it of thee at a price: neither will I offer burnt-offerings unto the Lord my God of that which doth cost me nothing. So David bought the threshingfloor and the oxen for fifty shekels of silver. And David built there an altar unto the Lord, and offered burnt-offerings and peace-offerings."—II Sam. 24:24,25.

And so the plague was stayed.

Ah, God had great things in mind for this place of sacrifice.

3. Here on Mount Moriah, on the Site of the Threshing Floor of Araunah or Ornan the Jebusite, Solomon Built the Temple of God

In II Chronicles 3:1 the Scripture says, "Then Solomon began

Under the golden dome is the rock where tradition says Abraham offered Isaac.

to build the house of the Lord at Jerusalem in mount Moriah, where the Lord appeared unto David his father, in the place that David had prepared in the threshingfloor of Ornan the Jebusite."

So here the worship of Israel was established in the beautiful Temple; here God set apart this place to be before Him "perpetually." And that rich Temple for which David had been saving up millions of dollars became one of the great buildings of the world. There were the sacrifices offered for sin and the Jews were not allowed to kill their sacrifices anywhere else.

The Dome of the Rock is now over what was thought to be the place of sacrifice. And inside that beautiful building a colorful wall encircles the rock that is said to be the very rock upon which Abraham was about to sacrifice Isaac!

Of course, we do not know that the tradition is true, and we do not know that Abraham built his altar upon a rock. But the Arabs think so. And this rock has a great hole in it where it is said the blood of the sacrifices of the Temple was poured and drained underground outside the city. That rock is counted sacred.

Just exactly where the holy place and the holy of holies were we do not know, but we know the general area, and the Temple was built on this site. It may well be that the great brass altar was beside this rock.

4. But Mount Moriah Is the Hill Upon Which the Saviour Was Crucified

Mount Moriah is a ridge that runs through the city of Jerusalem. One end of it juts up near the southeast corner of the city wall, and there the Temple stands. But the ridge runs on through Jerusalem to the north side, and on the north side, centuries before Christ, either Solomon or the Maccabees cut a great gap through the hill to make the wall safer, and there is a street. But the remnant of the hill Moriah juts up facing the city and the cut face of it has depressions and caves that sometimes look like the face of a skull.

There is Calvary, the place of a skull. As far as we know, that is the very hill upon which Jesus was crucified. And God had planned so long ago this holy mountain, this place where Abraham would offer his son picturing the Saviour and then the place where David would select as a place of sacrifice, and then the place where Solomon's Temple would be built. And on the same hill, a little ways away, would be the place of Calvary where Jesus was crucified! Just a little below that face like a skull is a garden, and there is a tomb cut back into the solid rock and that, we think, was Joseph's tomb where the Saviour was buried and from which He arose from the dead.

Ah, then, Mount Moriah has marvelous meaning and interest for all of us.

II. WHEN IS THAT TEMPLE TO BE REBUILT?

God had said to Solomon, "I have heard thy prayer and thy supplication, that thou hast made before me: I have hallowed this house, which thou hast built, to put my name there for ever; and mine eyes and mine heart shall be there perpetually."

Since God's eyes and heart are to be forever centered on Mount Moriah, and He has put His name there forever, surely God expects some future use of this hill and some Temple to be built there for His service.

1. But No Temple of God Is to Be Built There at This Present Time

Someone hopefully started a rumor that plans were already drawn for the rebuilding of the Temple in Jerusalem, limestone has already been purchased from Indiana and was being prepared. That is foolish and untrue. There are several reasons why.

In the first place, there are millions of Arabs and here on the site of Solomon's Temple is their most beautiful mosque in the world and the second most important. To them Jerusalem and the mosques here are second only to Mecca in importance. And two and a half million Jews could not, with the opposition of 700 million Arabs, rebuild a Temple here destroying the present mosques and taking charge of what Arabs themselves count holy ground. No, that is not reasonable.

Then the Jews themselves do not have the disposition nor the means and knowledge to rebuild the Temple. The Jews are unsaved. They do not know the Lord. The Jews are still in the same rebellion and unbelief for which they were scattered over all the world in the year A. D. 70, when Titus destroyed Jerusalem. They have no priesthood. They do not have the genealogy of the priests and have no way to find out. Most Jews do not even know from what tribe they came or whether from mixed blood.

The group of Orthodox Jews in Jerusalem generally are not even allowed to go upon this platform, the site of the Temple, but instead they wail at the west wall of the Temple site. They do not know just where was dedicated the holy place and the Mosaic law decreed death for anybody but an authorized priest to come into the holy place. They do not have the disposition to do so nor the understanding nor the unity of heart about it if they wanted

Entering the Temple area; the Dome of the Rock

to. No, they cannot and will not now build a temple in Jerusalem.

If there were a great turning to God with penitent hearts and seeking the Saviour, then someone might want a temple. And there is more limestone in Palestine than in Indiana, beautiful limestone. The rumor is foolish.

2. The Jews Will Have Some Kind of Holy Place in the Great Tribulation Time

In II Thessalonians, chapter 2, we are told about this Man of Sin, the Wicked, who will one day make himself known. But he cannot appear before the rapture. The mystery of iniquity already works, but the influence of the Holy Spirit through the mass of Christian people on earth prevents his appearing until after the rapture. Then when Christians are taken away and that dominant influence of the Holy Spirit that restrains him is removed, the Man of Sin will appear.

". . . and that man of sin be revealed, the son of perdition; Who opposeth and exalteth himself above all that is called God, or that is worshipped; so that he as God sitteth in the temple of God, shewing himself that he is God."—II Thess. 2:3,4.

Daniel 9:27 foretells that prince that shall come: "And he shall confirm the covenant with many for one week: and in the midst of the week he shall cause the sacrifice and the oblation to cease, and for the overspreading of abominations he shall make it desolate, even until the consummation, and that determined shall be poured upon the desolate." So the last half of the seven-year week, that is, three and a half years, the Man of Sin will be reigning and he will enter some kind of a temple claiming to be God and cause the sacrifices to cease. That is the "abomination of desolation, spoken of by Daniel the prophet" and foretold by the Lord Jesus in Matthew 24:15-21.

We can see that this will be in the tribulation time, after the rapture. We are not told that whatever temple the Jews have then will be on the site of Solomon's Temple; it may be, because the worldwide ruler could enforce it and build a temple there which could not be built now under the circumstances.

But Jews are planning now, we are told, to build a great synagogue in the Jerusalem area but not on the Temple site, and not as a place of sacrifices. It may be that in the tribulation time some such place will be turned into a temple and the Antichrist could designate somebody to be priest as heathen rulers have done before, and he could then violate that temple, claiming to be God on earth, as the Scripture says he will. But that is not until the tribulation time.

3. In the Kingdom Age Ezekiel Foretells Another Great Temple of God Here

The Lord has foretold that after the rapture and after the tribulation God will regather Israel. In Matthew 24:29-31 He said:

"Immediately after the tribulation of those days shall the sun be darkened, and the moon shall not give her light, and the stars shall fall from heaven, and the powers of the heavens shall be shaken: And then shall appear the sign of the Son of man in heaven: and then shall all the tribes of the earth mourn, and they shall see the Son of man coming in the clouds of heaven with power and great glory. And he shall send his angels with a great sound of a trumpet, and they shall gather together his elect from the four winds, from one end of heaven to the other."

In Deuteronomy 30:1-6 it was foretold that the Lord Himself would return and that Israel would turn to seek the Lord with all their heart and be circumcised of heart and He would gather them back to Palestine. In Ezekiel 20 it is foretold that He will take them to the wilderness of wanderings and purge out the rebels. In Zechariah we are told that "they shall look on him whom they pierced" and a nation will be converted in a day, as foretold in John 19:37 and Romans 11:26. Ezekiel 34 tells of that regathering of Jews from all the nations of the earth, and Ezekiel 36:24-28 gives some wonderfully sweet details:

"For I will take you from among the heathen, and gather you out of all countries, and will bring you into your own land. Then will I sprinkle clean water upon you, and ye shall be clean: from all your filthiness, and from all your idols, will I cleanse you. A

new heart also will I give you, and a new spirit will I put within you: and I will take away the stony heart out of your flesh, and I will give you an heart of flesh. And I will put my spirit within you, and cause you to walk in my statutes, and ye shall keep my judgments, and do them. And ye shall dwell in the land that I gave to your fathers; and ye shall be my people, and I will be your God."

Then, with Israel back in the land, and the rebels purged out, people loving and believing in the Lord Jesus as their King will need a Temple. So Ezekiel, chapters 40 to 44, tells the story of that Temple in Jerusalem.

III. THE MILLENNIAL TEMPLE WILL PASS AWAY FOR A BETTER TEMPLE

In I Corinthians 15:22-26 we read:

"For as in Adam all die, even so in Christ shall all be made alive. But every man in his own order: Christ the firstfruits; afterward they that are Christ's at his coming. Then cometh the end, when he shall have delivered up the kingdom to God, even the Father; when he shall have put down all rule and all authority and power. For he must reign, till he hath put all enemies under his feet. The last enemy that shall be destroyed is death."

1. Christ's Millennial Reign Covers Only One Thousand Years

Now why is the reign of Christ on earth limited to one thousand years? Why a new dispensation? And why a great change in Heaven and earth?

We remember that when Christ returns to reign, there will be people on earth with natural bodies and we suppose they will grow into unconverted sinners. Perhaps they are the children of some who are to be alive on earth and are to be kept alive because they have trusted Christ during the tribulation time and so they are received into the kingdom in Matthew 25:31-46. Then these unsaved people grow up and Christ will be reigning on the earth. God will be giving mankind another chance!

We are told of that millennial reign, "And the Lord shall be king over all the earth: in that day shall there be one Lord, and his name one" (Zech. 14:9). And then we are told:

"And it shall some to pass, that every one that is left of all the nations which came against Jerusalem shall even go up from year to year to worship the King, the Lord of hosts, and to keep the feast of tabernacles. And it shall be, that whoso will not come up of all the families of the earth unto Jerusalem to worship the King, the Lord of hosts, even upon them shall be no rain."— Zech. 14:16,17.

But even in the world with Christ reigning and perfect government and with the sacrifices at Jerusalem picturing the Gospel, as the Lord's Supper does now, and the feast of tabernacles with its sweet message of deliverance from evil and from sin, then people will rebel. Revelation 20:7-10—John saw this in a vision as if it had already happened:

"And when the thousand years are expired, Satan shall be loosed out of his prison, And shall go out to deceive the nations which are in the four quarters of the earth, Gog and Magog, to gather them together to battle: the number of whom is as the sand of the sea. And they went up on the breadth of the earth, and compassed the camp of the saints about, and the beloved city: and fire came down from God out of heaven, and devoured them. And the devil that deceived them was cast into the lake of fire and brimstone, where the beast and the false prophet are, and shall be tormented day and night for ever and ever."

2. But the Last Enemy to Be Destroyed Is Death
Now here comes the death of all those who rebelled, all those yet unsaved in the millennial earth, it seems. But the thousand years are ended and the last testing of mankind is done, and now out in space God sets up a great white throne and Christ is the Judge. And the 20th chapter of Revelation tells us how the unsaved are brought out of Hell, and death and Hell deliver up the dead that are in them and the sea delivers up the dead in it and they are judged every one according to their works. And then the last of these are sent back to Hell forever, both soul and body,

"And whosoever was not found written in the book of life was cast into the lake of fire."

But while that judgment of unsaved men of the ages is being done out in space, God will cleanse this creation which has been cursed by man's sin: "But the heavens and the earth, which are now, by the same word are kept in store, reserved unto fire against the day of judgment and perdition of ungodly men" (II Pet. 3:7). And then following that, verses 10-12 continue:

"But the day of the Lord will come as a thief in the night; in the which the heavens shall pass away with a great noise, and the elements shall melt with fervent heat, the earth also and the works that are therein shall be burned up. Seeing then that all these things shall be dissolved, what manner of persons ought ye to be in all holy conversation and godliness, Looking for and hasting unto the coming of the day of God, wherein the heavens being on fire shall be dissolved, and the elements shall melt with fervent heat?"

3. The Earth Made New

And now the last enemy to be destroyed is death and Christ has finished it. And now Christ is ready to turn the kingdom over to the Father and at long, long last the perfection of fellowship with God and man has been completed! So Revelation 21:1-5 tells us:

"And I saw a new heaven and a new earth: for the first heaven and the first earth were passed away; and there was no more sea. And I John saw the holy city, new Jerusalem, coming down from God out of heaven, prepared as a bride adorned for her husband. And I heard a great voice out of heaven saying, Behold, the tabernacle of God is with men, and he will dwell with them, and they shall be his people, and God himself shall be with them, and be their God. And God shall wipe away all tears from their eyes; and there shall be no more death, neither sorrow, nor crying, neither shall there be any more pain: for the former things are passed away. And he that sat upon the throne said, Behold, I make all things new. And he said unto me, Write: for these words are true and faithful."

Now, here is a new Garden of Eden on the earth. Everything that fire would melt is melted. All the marks of sin on this earth are destroyed. God can still keep His promise to Abraham, for the earth is still here in the land that was in the covenant. And now the Heavenly City itself comes down from God to be the Capital City of the earth, and God Himself takes over the kingdom.

IV. BUT WHERE IS THE TEMPLE?

When this earth is destroyed by fire, that millennial Temple will surely be destroyed also. What then? Well, in this new Heaven and this new earth we find, "Behold, the tabernacle of God is with men, and he will dwell with them, and they shall be his people, and God himself shall be with them, and be their God" (Rev. 21:3). We will not then need a church house or a Temple, for we will have God Himself right in the midst of us. God and Christ and all Heaven itself will be ours!

1. Can Any Earthly House Built by Men Contain God?

Ah, Solomon saw so well that any temple on earth is not sufficient for God. He said, when he dedicated the Temple at Jerusalem, "But will God in very deed dwell with men on the earth? behold, heaven and the heaven of heavens cannot contain thee; how much less this house which I have built!" (II Chron. 6:18).

You see, a Temple on earth could only be a reminder, a type of the presence of God. It never was sufficient.

And so now, when Heaven comes down to earth and God Himself abides forever with men, not far off, not in the holy place of the Temple set off from all the common people, but in the happy, most intimate presence of all His people in the world, then there will be no need for a temple made with hands.

2. God Himself and Christ Are the Temple Then

John looked at that wonderful Heavenly City, the New Jerusalem, the new center and capital of the new world—he looked on it with amazement. There was no more sea. There was no more night, for nobody is ever tired to need rest. Of course, there was no prison, for no one will ever sin there. And he saw the marvels of the gates of pearl and the great wall, high, and the twelve gates, the gold-paved streets and the precious stones, in that city foursquare. And then he said:

"And I saw no temple therein: for the Lord God Almighty and the Lamb are the temple of it. And the city had no need of the sun, neither of the moon, to shine in it: for the glory of God did lighten it, and the Lamb is the light thereof."—Rev. 21:22,23.

Oh, God, our Temple, it is in Thee we dwell.

There was a little picture of this in the mind of David the psalmist when he spoke of dwelling "in the secret place of the most High," and when he said, "I will dwell in the house of the Lord for ever" (Ps. 23:6). And Jesus gave a hint of it when He told the longing of His heart over Jerusalem and wept as He said it: "How often would I have gathered thy children together, as a hen doth gather her brood under her wings, and ye would not!"

Ah, the Lord God Himself and the Lamb will be the Temple and there will be no more need for a temple then, no need for sacrifices, no need for ceremonies, no need for pictures. We will have the Lord Himself and God the Father in the most intimate, eternal blessedness of fellowship.

V. NOW THE BODY OF THE CHRISTIAN IS THE TEMPLE OF GOD

Very often the church auditorium is called "the sanctuary." That is not only untrue but it is almost blasphemous.

1. No Church Building Is the Temple of God

God does not live in church houses. People try to cultivate "reverence for the house of God." There is nothing like that in the Bible. It is true that the minor prophet Habakkuk says, "The Lord is in his holy temple: let all the earth keep silence before him" (2:20). Yes, when the Lord dwelt in a holy place, the Shekinah Glory in the holy of holies of the Temple at Jerusalem, the Lord was in His Temple in that sense.

But that is not true now. When Jerusalem was destroyed and

the Temple was destroyed, the Lord had foretold, "Behold, your house is left unto you desolate." And the Temple? In the sense of a holy place, set apart for God, there is no Temple, no building in the world that is a Temple. We may call it that and it comes to mean only a house, but it is not a Temple in any real sense.

It is remarkable that in all the New Testament there is not the mention of a single church building. They may have built church buildings to worship in. They would need meeting places. But if they did it is never mentioned, because God wants to keep it clear that places are not holy.

I think we ought to respect others when we are in public services, and we ought to have respect for the Word of God which is being read or preached, but there is no need to make a big to-do of worshiping a church house. That does not please God.

2. The Lord Jesus Made This Clear to the Woman of Samaria

In John 4 the woman of Samaria thought, "You Jews think the only place to worship God is in Jerusalem. I'll tell You that the synagogue here on Mount Gerizim is just as good." And Jesus told her:

"Woman, believe me, the hour cometh, when ye shall neither in this mountain, nor yet at Jerusalem, worship the Father. Ye worship ye know not what: we know what we worship: for salvation is of the Jews. But the hour cometh, and now is, when the true worshippers shall worship the Father in spirit and in truth: for the Father seeketh such to worship him. God is a Spirit: and they that worship him must worship him in spirit and in truth. The woman saith unto him, I know that Messias cometh, which is called Christ: when he is come, he will tell us all things."

Oh, what God wants is heart worship. Not the ceremonies of a place, nor incense on the altar, but the love and praise from godly hearts and loving hearts. He wants devotion and praise for the blood Christ shed and a holy confidence that that pays everything instead of our offering blood of bulls and goats. Now the temple of God is in the heart of a Christian.

3. The Holy Spirit Makes the Christian's Body His Temple

Remember in John 14:16,17 Jesus said:

"And I will pray the Father, and he shall give you another Comforter, that he may abide with you for ever; Even the Spirit of truth; whom the world cannot receive, because it seeth him not, neither knoweth him: but ye know him; for he dwelleth with you, and shall be in you."

Will you notice the Lord said, ". . . ye know him; for he dwelleth WITH you, and shall be IN you." The Holy Spirit was with the disciples until Christ rose from the dead. Then, after the resurrection, the Holy Spirit was in them. That is the meaning of John 7:37-39:

"In the last day, that great day of the feast, Jesus stood and cried, saying, If any man thirst, let him come unto me, and drink. He that believeth on me, as the scripture hath said, out of his belly shall flow rivers of living water. (But this spake he of the Spirit, which they that believe on him should receive: for the Holy Ghost was not yet given; because that Jesus was not yet glorified.)"

So in John 20, the day Jesus arose from the dead, He came to the disciples. "Then said Jesus to them again, Peace be unto you: as my Father hath sent me, even so send I you. And when he had said this, he breathed on them, and saith unto them, Receive ye the Holy Ghost" (21,22).

The Holy Spirit moved in that day into the bodies of Christians everywhere.

Now Jesus is glorified, and the Holy Spirit is given to abide in the bodies of Christians.

So I Corinthians 6:19,20 explains: "What? know ye not that your body is the temple of the Holy Ghost which is in you, which ye have of God, and ye are not your own? For ye are bought with a price: therefore glorify God in your body, and in your spirit, which are God's."

And Romans 8:9 says: "But ye are not in the flesh, but in the Spirit, if so be that the Spirit of God dwell in you. Now if any many have not the Spirit of Christ, he is none of his."

So every Christian now has the Holy Spirit within. The body of a Christian is the temple of God on earth, not any church building, not any denominational headquarters. Christ Himself within a Christian through the indwelling Holy Spirit is the temple today.

So we should present our bodies a living sacrifice. So we should put on the new man and day by day live as one who is in truth the habitation of God on earth and the representative of God on earth.

Oh, yon site of Solomon's Temple! I have a better temple than that which reared its gilded towers here. I have God in my heart. My sins are forgiven. I am an heir of God, a joint heir with Christ, and the Father and the Son both manifest Themselves in me. I am God's temple.

VIII. With Jesus, Moses and Elijah
on the Mount of Transfiguration

Our buses have brought us from Jerusalem north through
Samaria into the Valley of Jezreel, also called the Valley of
Megiddo or Esdraelon. Now we see on ahead, rising out of the
valley, a round mountain. It is shaped like a big bowl turned up-
side down, standing alone, not part of a range of mountains. It is
Mount Tabor, which tradition says is the Mount of Transfiguration.

The buses follow a continually rising road around the side of
the mountain till we park, only a little way up. Now the road is
too steep and the hairpin turns so narrow for the buses, so we
have arranged for many taxicabs to meet us here. We load up,
five to a car, and take that steep road to the top.

1. Is Mount Tabor the Site of the Transfiguration?

Is this mountain actually the place of the transfiguration,
where Jesus was transformed into heavenly glory, where Moses
and Elijah appeared, and where God spoke aloud, "This is my
beloved Son: hear him" (Mark 9:7)? We think it may be, but
God has chosen that we cannot know for certain, perhaps, lest we
should tend to worship the place instead of rejoicing in the event
and the revelation concerning it.

All the Scriptures say about the place is, "And after six days
Jesus taketh Peter, James, and John his brother, and bringeth
them up into an high mountain apart" (Matt. 17:1). No further
identification of the mountain is given.

Some people think the transfiguration occurred on Mount Hermon or another peak some distance north of the Sea of Galilee. Hermon is that highest mountain in the area, and is snow-capped, being over 8,000 feet high, perhaps 25 miles or more north of Capernaum and the Sea of Galilee. They think this may be the place, or some other peak in that northern area, because Jesus had been at Caesarea Philippi a week or so before and Caesarea Philippi is not far from Mount Hermon, and there Peter had made that great confession, "Thou art the Christ, the Son of the living God" (Matt. 16:13-16).

2. Compare Arguments for Hermon, for Tabor

But that was "about an eight days after these sayings," Luke 9:28 says, or "after six days," that is, more than six days, as Matthew and Mark say it, about eight days after the Lord Jesus' visit to Caesarea Philippi. He may have stayed in that area for a week, but it is not described. In that time He could well have come perhaps the forty miles south by the Sea of Galilee and to Mount Tabor.

Mount Tabor, supposed Mount of Transfiguration

Around Mount Hermon was Gentile territory where Jesus was not so likely to spend much time. And the crowd that gathered at the foot of the mountain after Jesus came down seems to have been a Jewish crowd, familiar with His marvelous works. And as Jesus walked and talked He may have come back in those eight days' time to the area with which He was more familiar and where He visited often, to towns such as Nazareth, Cana and Nain.

Mount Hermon was high, with a snow-capped top. Jesus went to the mount "to pray." But Mount Hermon, over 8,000 feet high, would take a day or two of hard climbing. Why would Jesus go up there amid the snow to pray? And why in this Gentile area?

Mount Tabor is a lower mountain. It could be climbed in a few hours. It would have space and privacy for the time of prayer. It was in the area Jesus most often visited. And so tradition points to Mount Tabor as the site of the transfiguration. At any rate, it will represent that to us, as we visit it, look out over the valley, remember the marvelous teaching Jesus gave about the transfiguration itself.

There is a Catholic church on top in memory of the transfiguration. Monks and nuns there run the refreshment stand and feed tourists and sell pictures and slides. A Father Joseph, there for some years, met us. He was an American, and a beautiful musician. He played and sang old hymns for us. He left, and I think it was the last time we saw him there, he said earnestly, "Please pray for me."

I. JESUS WAS HERE TRANSFIGURED

In Matthew 16:28 Jesus promised the disciples, "Verily I say unto you, There be some standing here, which shall not taste of death, till they see the Son of man coming in his kingdom." Then follows the account of the transfiguration, beginning the next chapter. "And after six days Jesus taketh Peter, James and John his brother, and bringeth them up into an high mountain apart, And was transfigured before them: and his face did shine as the sun, and his raiment was white as the light" (Matt. 17:1,2).

1. He Assumes for a Bit His Heavenly Form

There are many evidences that Jesus felt some homesickness for Heaven and looked forward with great joy to the time when He would be glorified again. He mentioned it several times. And in John 17:4,5 Jesus, in His high priestly prayer, said, "I have glorified thee on the earth: I have finished the work which thou gavest me to do. And now, O Father, glorify thou me with thine own self with the glory which I had with thee before the world was." He prayed for that glory and was answered in John 12:28, "Father, glorify thy name. Then came there a voice from heaven, saying, I have both glorified it, and will glorify it again."

I can imagine that a king, traveling incognito, in disguise as a common person, traveling around to learn what he can, if he is long away from palace and home, must be glad to get back to the familiar honor of his palace and the love of his servants and subjects.

We know that Jesus gave Himself with all His heart to fulfilling His work to die for sinners. But we would understand that His loving heart longed to see the face of the Father and enter into the glory He had had with the Father before the world began.

Now on the Mount of Transfiguration He illustrates how His glory will be. When John saw the resurrected Saviour who gave him the inspired book of Revelation, John said:

"And in the midst of the seven candlesticks one like unto the Son of man, clothed with a garment down to the foot, and girt about the paps with a golden girdle. His head and his hairs were white like wool, as white as snow; and his eyes were as a flame of fire; And his feet like unto fine brass, as if they burned in a furnace; and his voice as the sound of many waters. And he had in his right hand seven stars: and out of his mouth went a sharp twoedged sword: and his countenance was as the sun shineth in his strength. And when I saw him, I fell at his feet as dead. And he laid his right hand upon me, saying unto me, Fear not; I am the first and the last: I am he that liveth, and was dead; and, behold, I am alive for evermore, Amen; and have the keys of hell and of death."—Rev. 1:13-18.

This is Jesus who, on the Mount of Transfiguration, gives us a little glimpse of His glory.

2. But This Is a Picture of Christ at His Second Coming

In Matthew 16:28 Jesus said, "Verily I say unto you, There be some standing here, which shall not taste of death, till they see the Son of man coming in his kingdom." So these disciples were promised that before they died they would "see the Son of man coming in his kingdom." This is what Jesus meant. This is how Jesus will appear when He comes back to reign on the earth.

Peter was inspired to write:

"For we have not followed cunningly devised fables, when we made known unto you the power and coming of our Lord Jesus Christ, but were eyewitnesses of his majesty. For he received from God the Father honour and glory, when there came such a voice to him from the excellent glory, This is my beloved Son, in whom I am well pleased. And this voice which came from heaven we heard, when we were with him in the holy mount."—II Pet. 1:16-18.

Ah, how Peter remembered that "holy mount" where he had seen the Saviour in resurrection glory! And Peter was not witnessing then of hearsay but was an eyewitness of the glory of Christ. And it is Christ in His kingdom who is so pictured here.

3. This Then Pictures the Reigning Christ in Glory and Judgment After Suffering

John in Revelation tells of the return of Christ in glory. It will be after the rapture of the saints, after the tribulation time on earth, and after our meeting at the judgment seat of Christ in Heaven, when Christ will come back with saints and angels to the world. This is pictured in Revelation 19:11-16:

"And I saw heaven opened, and behold a white horse; and he that sat upon him was called Faithful and True, and in righteousness he doth judge and make war. His eyes were as a flame of fire, and on his head were many crowns; and he had a name written, that no man knew, but he himself. And he was clothed with a vesture dipped in blood: and his name is called

The Word of God. And the armies which were in heaven followed him upon white horses, clothed in fine linen, white and clean. And out of his mouth goeth a sharp sword, that with it he should smite the nations: and he shall rule them with a rod of iron: and he treadeth the winepress of the fierceness and wrath of Almighty God. And he hath on his vesture and on his thigh a name written, KING OF KINGS, AND LORD OF LORDS."

There we see Christ with a sword. We saw Him in the Gospels as a suffering Saviour, despised and rejected, crucified. Now we see Him in resurrection glory, coming with a sword and with the armies of Heaven. And He treads out the winepress of the destruction of His enemies and the blood will rise, in that battle of Armageddon, to the bridles of the horses.

Then will come the time when "the kingdoms of this world are become the kingdoms of our Lord, and of his Christ" (Rev. 11:15). Then will be fulfilled the picture seen by Nebuchadnezzar in a dream of a great statue representing the empires of this world and a stone cut out of a mountain rolls down crashing into these kingdoms, grinding them to powder. So Christ will take over all the kingdoms of this world when He comes back to reign.

This same Christ is the One who will judge the world. All judgment is given into His hands. Revelation 20:11 speaks of it: "And I saw a great white throne, and him that sat on it, from whose face the earth and the heaven fled away; and there was found no place for them."

And Daniel 7:9,10 speaks of it also in these words:

"I beheld till the thrones were cast down, and the Ancient of days did sit, whose garment was white as snow, and the hair of his head like the pure wool: his throne was like the fiery flame, and his wheels as burning fire. A fiery stream issued and came forth from before him: thousand thousands ministered unto him, and ten thousand times ten thousand stood before him: the judgment was set, and the books were opened."

Jesus is pictured as the coming King and Judge.

II. MOSES AND ELIJAH MEET JESUS

"And, behold, there appeared unto them Moses and Elias

talking with him. Then answered Peter, and said unto Jesus,
Lord, it is good for us to be here: if thou wilt, let us make here
three tabernacles; one for thee, and one for Moses, and one for
Elias. While he yet spake, behold, a bright cloud overshadowed
them: and behold a voice out of the cloud, which said, This is my
beloved Son, in whom I am well pleased; hear ye him. And when
the disciples heard it, they fell on their face, and were sore afraid.
And Jesus came and touched them, and said, Arise, and be not
afraid. And when they had lifted up their eyes, they saw no man,
save Jesus only."—Matt. 17:3-8.

It is such a short step from Heaven to earth. All about us are
the angels of God who go to Heaven to report and are back to be
servants and ministers of those who are to believe. And Jacob,
the fleeing young man at Bethel, found "the Lord is in this place;
and. . .knew it not." Hagar, thinking she would see her boy
starve in the wilderness, found God was there and said, "Thou
God seest me."

So Moses and Elijah came to meet Jesus on the Mount of
Transfiguration.

1. They Represented the Law and the Prophets

The law was written by Moses, who could so well picture the
law. Moses came to meet Jesus here. He had written about Him
so many times. Oh, how it must have burned in the heart of
Moses as he had revealed to him that the blood of the perfect
lamb on the door was the only hope to escape judgment in Egypt!
And as they roasted the male lamb of the first year, without
blemish, roasted it whole with fire and no water, and eaten with
bitter herbs, he surely knew about the suffering Saviour who
would die, the Innocent for the guilty, to pay for our sins.

Oh, Moses remembered the serpent God had him put up on a
pole, a brazen, shiny serpent, and whosoever looked at that serpent was healed of snakebite. And he knew John 3:16 evidently,
just as those who look at Christ on the cross are saved.

He knew about that great rock in the desert and that smitten
rock poured out a river of life-giving water for three and a half
million people and their animals. And that rock was Christ.

The chapel on Mount Tabor

He knew all the sacrifices and the priesthood picturing Jesus. And the manna from Heaven picturing Christ, the Bread of Life. And the golden candlestick, or lampstand, burning beaten olive oil, picturing Christ filled with the Spirit as the Light of the world. Yes, Moses could properly come to represent the law before Jesus.

You can make sure that means not that the law ever saved anybody but the law pointed to Jesus. "Wherefore the law was our schoolmaster to bring us unto Christ" (Gal. 3:24).

Moses was saved by faith in the coming Saviour and that was the meaning of all the law and symbols and ceremonies. As Colossians 2:17 says, "Which are a shadow of things to come; but the body is of Christ."

And here is Elijah, too, a representative of the prophets. What a marvelous ministry this mighty man had! Almost alone, in a nation given over to idolatry, how bold was his preaching, his praying! How great was the blessing of God upon him at Mount

Carmel and elsewhere! Now he comes to represent the prophets with Jesus.

Remember Acts 10:43 says, "To him give all the prophets witness, that through his name whosoever believeth in him shall receive remission of sins." Every prophet in the Old Testament—Elijah and the rest of them—pictured Christ as the suffering Saviour and that one who trusted Him is saved. It is in the Old Testament we are told, ". . .the just shall live by his faith" (Hab. 2:4). It is in Isaiah that we learn about the virgin birth and the suffering of the Saviour and atonement. And all the prophets pointed toward the Saviour Himself and the wonderful salvation that no one could ever have except as he comes to know and trust the Saviour. So Abraham did and so did all the prophets.

Moses said this about Jesus, "A prophet shall the Lord your God raise up unto you of your brethren, like unto me; him shall ye hear in all things whatsoever he shall say unto you" (Deut. 18:15,19; Acts 3:22).

2. The Cloud on the Mount of Transfiguration Was Associated With Christ's Second Coming

Isn't it interesting that Matthew 17:5 tells us, "While he yet spake, behold, a bright cloud overshadowed them: and behold a voice out of the cloud, which said, This is my beloved Son, in whom I am well pleased; hear ye him."

We remember when Jesus ascended to Heaven from the Mount of Olives: "While they beheld, he was taken up; and a cloud received him out of their sight" (Acts 1:9). And Revelation 1:7, of the Second Coming, says, "Behold, he cometh with clouds; and every eye shall see him, and they also which pierced him: and all kindreds of the earth shall wail because of him. Even so, Amen."

Jesus left from the Mount of Olives (Acts 1:12). He will return to the Mount of Olives when He comes to reign, after the rapture, for Zechariah 14:4 says, "And his feet shall stand in that day upon the mount of Olives, which is before Jerusalem on the east."

3. Oh, but Peter, Do Not Promote Moses or Elijah but Jesus Only

Peter was confused: "For he wist not what to say; for they were sore afraid," Mark tells us. But he said, "Lord, it is good for us to be here: if thou wilt, let us make here three tabernacles; one for thee, and one for Moses, and one for Elias." Ah, Peter, that is a mistake. It is a tremendous mistake to put Moses, Elijah and Jesus on the same plane. Moses would be on his face before the Lord Jesus. Elijah the prophet would be before Him like any other redeemed sinner. Jesus is God. And no one ought ever be put on an equal with Him.

The sin of Romanism is to put Mary as a mediatrix and teach people to pray to Mary, asking her to intercede and calling her the Queen of Heaven. That is a mistake of all those who put some tradition, some church creed, in authority except the words of Christ and the Bible. So, if you make a tabernacle for Jesus, do not make a tabernacle for Moses and Elijah.

When Peter, speaking in confusion because he didn't know what to say, suggested three tabernacles, suddenly the place was enshrouded with a cloud from Heaven. And then Moses and Elijah were gone and when the cloud removed there was only Jesus, and the voice from Heaven said, "THIS is my beloved Son. . . hear ye him"!

Jesus is not merely a great man or great prophet, He is God incarnate, the only begotten Son of God, Creator, our only Saviour. Do not count Jesus with the great of the earth. Do not put any other beside Him.

III. BUT THE LORD JESUS MUST GO BACK TO THE TROUBLED WORLD BELOW

Peter suggested that they simply stay on top of the mount, in that holy place, with the company of Moses and Elijah! But He was wrong.

1. The Lord Jesus Does Not Call Anyone to the Life of a Hermit and Secret Holiness

How like the Apostle Peter many others are! They seek the "deeper life." They gather in Bible study classes.

In old times, a monk built a column some thirty feet high and lived upon that, hoping thus to escape the contamination of the world and be holy. He was wrong.

Many a monk thinks that to wear sackcloth, to go barefoot or with pebbles in their shoes, even to scourge themselves to humiliate the flesh, they thus become holy. They are wrong.

Before he was converted, John Wesley gave up so many things and earnestly tried to humble the flesh, but not until he was converted and had upon him the power of God and gave in to soul winning was he in the real will of God for him.

Madam Guyon tells much of her subjective seeking to be holy, to give away even her children and avoid the duties she had as a mother, and to do everything required by the Catholic Church and archbishops. But what God wants a Christian to do is to stand between God and the poor sinning world.

Down below the mountain is a devil-possessed boy. He has been that way from childhood. Demons cast him into the fire or into the water to drown. The father is desperate. He brought the lad to the eight apostles of the Lord there—but they could not heal him. Jesus must go back to that troubled crowd. The apostles must go, too!

The other day I was told about a church where the pastor insists that no church should have over 300 members. It should give itself more to studying the Word and trying to draw near to God. But that man would be greatly embarrassed, would he not, at Pentecost, with 3,000 saved in a day, then other thousands day after day and multitudes, both of men and women?

They want fellowship with a choice little group of Christians.

And many people who seek the "deeper life" and attend Bible conferences never win a soul. They never lie awake at night weeping. They never wet pillows with tears over a dying world about them. Sometimes they do not win even their own loved ones or next-door neighbors. Any kind of holiness or "deeper life" that leaves out the one main thing for which Christ died—soul winning—is not good.

Christians do not need to build three tabernacles and stay on the Mount of Transfiguration. The Great Commission is for us to go into all the world and preach the Gospel to every creature. The last promise in the Bible admonishes us, "Let him that heareth say, Come." What a mistake it is for Christians to be self-centered in seeking for holiness or Bible knowledge without entering into the burden and compassion of Christ for a dying world!

Oh, let us come down from the Mount of Transfiguration to the heartbroken people below. It is good to have some time alone with Christ, but only good if we then set out to do what Jesus commands us to do and win the poor desolate sinner for Christ.

2. The Devil-Possessed Boy

The father had brought his troubled, devil-possessed son to the apostles below. They could not heal. They had been given power to cast out devils: why, then, could they not cast this one out? Jesus answered them, "Because of your unbelief. . .this kind goeth not out but by prayer and fasting."

Some have doubted whether that statement, "This kind goeth not out but by prayer and fasting," was in the original manuscript or had been added by some copyist. But whether it is added or not, this is the teaching of the Scripture elsewhere. To have the mighty power of God means waiting on God and turning our hearts and minds away from the ordinary comforts and pleasures of this life. Those who wait upon God can have His power. God does not give faith to the careless and indifferent heart.

The father now wondered if Jesus could heal, since the apostles had failed. He said, "If thou canst do any thing, have compassion on us, and help us." Jesus answered, "If thou canst believe, all things are possible to him that believeth." So Jesus cast out the devils and delivered the tormented child, now well, to his father.

Oh, thank God, Jesus did not go on to Heaven and leave us here until things were settled. He came down from the Mount of Transfiguration to finish the course God had set for Him and pay man's debt and conquer death for us.

And even now, thank God, He does not leave us alone but He

said, "Lo, I am with you alway, even unto the end of the world" (Matt. 28:20). And says Hebrews 13:5,6: "Let your conversation be without covetousness; and be content with such things as ye have: for he hath said, I will never leave thee, nor forsake thee. So that we may boldly say, The Lord is my helper, and I will not fear what man shall do unto me."

Oh, the dear Lord Jesus is available for all the broken hearts, all the devil-possessed sinners, all the troubled fathers and mothers, all the preachers who must have His help. Jesus came down from the Mount of Transfiguration; so we come down to go on with the work God has put upon us of getting out the Gospel to every creature.

IX. At Jericho With Jesus: We Meet Bartimaeus and Zacchaeus

Jericho is an ancient city in the valley of the Jordan River, a mile or two from the river. It was the first city to fall when Joshua and the children of Israel set out to conquer the land, coming across the Jordan River. It was the city of Rahab, a devoted convert who became great grandmother of King David.

Here is where Elisha cured the bitter waters of Jericho, which water still runs clear, sweet and good. Near here is where Naaman the Assyrian dipped seven times in the River Jordan and was healed of his leprosy.

This city Jesus passed through. On His last journey up to Jerusalem, He came down the Jordan River Valley to Jericho, then about twenty-two miles up the mountains and hills to Jerusalem. Jerusalem is about 2,500 feet above sea level. Jericho is 1,200 feet below sea level. So the Scripture speaks of a man who "went down to Jericho," and those who "went up to Jerusalem."

Near Jericho are the excavated ruins of the walls of Jericho, mounds and towers and surroundings of long ago. The guides have been taught to say that this was the "pre-Joshua walls of Jericho," but they are mistaken. A lady archaeologist, Dr. Kenyon, not believing the Bible account and Bible chronology, figured out that the Israelites came into this land a little more than 1200 B.C., so when she found artifacts here, going up to 1450 B.C., she supposed it was a pre-Israelitish civilization, one she thought was better than that of Israel. She was mistaken.

Israelites crossed the Jordan River after forty years in the desert about 1451 B.C., and the artifacts she found by digging in the ruins of the best civilization was of Israel itself.

West, toward Jerusalem, is what is traditionally called the "Mount of Temptation" where it is said Jesus stayed forty days and was tempted of the Devil. We have no historical proof that

Ancient wall of Jericho being excavated

this is the place but it was in some high mountain in Judaea and this may have been the mountain.

Jericho has wonderful trees and flowers. It has beautiful bougainvillaea and an abundance of oranges and bananas.

Perhaps two miles away is where the Jordan flows into the Dead Sea, with the saltiest sea water in the world, perhaps about 25% salt and minerals. No far away is the site where we think Jesus was baptized.

I. THE MIRACULOUS CONQUEST OF JERICHO

When the children of Israel crossed the Jordan River, they had wandered forty years in the wilderness since leaving Egypt. They did not make the most direct approach up from the south, through the country of the Philistines and by Hebron. Rather, they came around the Dead Sea and approached from the east. They had already had battles with the Amalekites, the Midianites, the Amorites and the Moabites, and had taken most of the east bank of the Jordan River and there would settle two and a half tribes. (The story of the fall of Jericho is told in Joshua, chapter 6).

1. God Had Put the Fear of Israel in the Canaanite Inhabitants of Palestine

The people of Jericho had heard of the plagues in Egypt, of the destruction of Pharaoh and his armies. They had heard of the marvelous leadership of God who fed the children of Israel manna from Heaven for forty years. They had heard of their successes against every group that came against them.

So when spies were sent across the Jordan into Jericho to spy out the land and bring Joshua word about how strong the city was and how they should go about taking it, the word went quickly to the king of Jericho that two men had come from hated Israel forces, and they were frightened. The two men went to the house of Rahab the harlot who hid them. And the king's soldiers sought in vain for these messengers.

2. God Had a Wonderful Plan for Taking the City

The children of Israel were commanded that the whole company should march around the city one day—everybody quietly. Then they should return to their camp. The second day, the third day, the fourth day, and on through until the seventh day, the whole of the nation were to march around the city once a day. On the seventh day they were to march around it seven times, then at a signal the trumpets were blown and there would be a mighty shout. So the people did and the walls fell down flat! Then they went over the fallen wall to take the city.

Since God was giving them power and destroyed the walls and defense of the city, it was clearly commanded that all the treasures in the city would belong to Him. But Achan stole some shekels of silver, a wedge of gold and a Babylonish garment, and hid them in his tent. We are told how God insisted they must search him out and bring him to judgment. And he and his family were stoned to death and buried in a canyon.

When they go to take this land of Canaan, they must remember that God is the One in charge and He is the One who gives them victory.

3. The Wonderful Story of Rahab

The Bible plainly says that Rahab was a harlot. It may be that in connection with her trade she ran an inn. Or it may be that since people generally knew about her house and she received many visitors, these spies found their way there.

But Rahab knew how God had been blessing Israel and bringing ruin to those who opposed Israel. So she hid the spies. Then she had them lie down on the rooftop and she covered them with stalks of flax until the danger was over. Then she requested that her father, mother, brothers and sisters should be spared the death that was certain to come to the opposing in Jericho. Would they spare them?

The spies made with her a solemn contract that if she would not tell of their presence nor their plans, all in her house would be spared. And she let down a scarlet cord from the window as a mark.

When the walls fell down, that house alone on the wall seemed to be spared, along with her people. And Rahab was taken into the nation Israel.

Not only is the story told in Joshua, chapter 2, but she is mentioned in Matthew 1:5, Hebrews 11:31 and in James 2:25. Hebrews 11:31 tells us, "By faith the harlot Rahab perished not with them that believed not, when she had received the spies with peace." So we know that she looked to the God of Israel and put her trust in Him.

She repeated to those spies all she had heard—"how the Lord dried up the water of the Red sea for you . . . and what ye did unto the two kings of the Amorites, that were on the other side Jordan, Sihon and Og, whom ye utterly destroyed." So she knew about the great God of Israel and, no doubt, knew about the Saviour who was promised and pictured in the types and sacrifices. And this woman who had been a harlot, now converted, married a Hebrew man, Salmon, and Matthew 1:5 tells us that she became the mother of Boaz, then Boaz married Ruth the Moabitess, and Jesse the father of David was born.

Ah, what wonderful honor came to Rahab! She was converted, her father and mother and brothers and sisters were spared, and she married into the ancestral line of the Lord Jesus Himself. She is listed in that Hebrews 11 Hall of Fame, where are the names of the mighty men and women of faith. James 2:25 tells how she was justified by her works, that is, proved to be a good believer.

Ah, sweet story of Rahab, the heathen woman, the harlot woman, who reached such heights of blessing!

We are reminded of Moses who was learned in all the wisdom of the Egyptians, yet he forsook Egypt and chose "rather to suffer affliction with the people of God, than to enjoy the pleasures of sin for a season."

II. ELISHA THE PROPHET LIVED AT JERICHO

We know that Elijah the prophet stayed about Samaria in the northern kingdom of Israel. He was once at Dothan. He prayed down the fire of God on sacrifices at Mount Carmel, near where Haifi is now. Then when Elijah was about to go to Heaven in a whirlwind with the chariot of fire, he went from Gilgal to Bethel, then to Jericho, then to Jordan. Elisha had so longed to have the mighty power of God. He pleaded that he might have a double portion of the Spirit of God that was on Elijah. It was promised that if he should be present when Elijah went to Heaven, he would get the mantle of Elijah and the power of God upon him— a double portion of the Spirit on Elisha. So he would not be distracted; he would not stop at Gilgal, nor Bethel, nor Jericho but on to cross the Jordan with Elijah.

Then when Elijah was taken to Heaven, his mantle fell and Elisha laid aside his garments and took up that mighty garment of Elijah. He wrapped it together and smote the waters of the Jordan and they opened before him as they had for Elijah.

The power of God was now on Elisha. Oh, what a blessing to have such power! And it may be a part of the answer to his prayer for a "double portion" of the Spirit that was on Elijah, that while Elijah had eight major miracles recorded, Elisha had sixteen major miracles recorded.

1. Elisha's Fountain Still Waters Jericho!

Then the men of the city of Jericho came to Elisha and said:

"Behold, I pray thee, the situation of this city is pleasant, as my lord seeth: but the water is naught, and the ground barren. And he said, Bring me a new cruse, and put salt therein. And they brought it to him. And he went forth unto the spring of the waters, and cast the salt in there, and said, Thus saith the Lord, I have healed these waters; there shall not be from thence any more death or barren land. So the waters were healed unto this day, according to the saying of Elisha which he spake."—II Kings 2:19-22.

I remember with joy the first time we drove up the street of Jericho, among the palm trees and flowering trees and shrubs, up toward the ruins of the old city. There beside the street ran a stream of water in a trough closed in by stones. It was about two feet wide and water was running three or four inches deep. When I called attention to it, I was told, "That is Elisha's fountain!" Now, after twenty-eight centuries the water still runs sweet and

Elisha's fountain, still flowing

good. In a moment's time the Lord changed whatever the mineral content of the water was—alkali or other distasteful and bad things—and now for twenty-eight centuries and more the miracle has continued.

Now I think they are piping the water out, but there it flows out in a pool and every year some of us drink water from Elisha's fountain and remember his blessings.

2. It Must Have Been Near Here Where Naaman the Syrian Was Healed of His Leprosy

Remember that Naaman was chief captain of the armies of Syria and lived in Damascus. He was a great man, "but he was a leper." And the Syrian armies had made raids into Israel and there had stolen away a little Israelite girl. But she loved the Lord and loved her master who had brought her, I suppose, as a slave girl to wait on his wife.

And the girl said to her mistress, "If my master were in Israel, we have there a prophet of God. He could be healed of his leprosy." The word got to Naaman and then to the king of Syria, and the king sent Naaman with a procession. He took with him gold and silver and beautiful garments as presents for the king, if the king would see that Naaman's leprosy were cured.

Naturally the king was astonished and half angry. Were they trying to provoke a war? What fools thought he could cure leprosy?

But the Prophet Elisha heard of it and said, "Send him to me." Now the little procession—the chariot of Naaman and his company—drove up before Elisha's house. Ah, Naaman thought Elisha would come with some palaver and ceremonies and with passing his hands over the afflicted portions, would some way cure his leprosy. But Elisha simply sent his servant to say, "Go and wash in Jordan seven times, and thy flesh shall come again to thee, and thou shalt be clean."

Naaman was angry. That seemed very slight respect for his prominence. What could the muddy waters of Jordan do, when they had better rivers in Damascus? But his servants prevailed upon him, so Naaman went to the Jordan and dipped—one time, twice, three times, four times, five times, six times, seven times!

After the seventh time, as he arose from the waters he found his skin was as fresh as a baby's. The leprosy was gone! How sweetly II Kings, chapter 5, tells it!

You remember that Elisha would take no reward for that wonderful miracle; and Naaman was evidently converted. Naaman said to Elisha that still when the king went to the house of Rimmon to worship, leaning on Naaman's arm, that he, as a general, ought to go with his king, but he would not worship there. He wanted two mules' burden of earth from Israel to go back so he would have a little place that was Israel in the midst of a foreign land, and there he could worship Israel's God!

I think that Naaman was wonderfully saved because of the testimony of a little Jewish girl and because of the power of God on this man Elisha.

Ah, Jericho was the center of many wonderful events.

III. THE LORD JESUS PASSED THROUGH JERICHO

There were two routes from the province of Galilee down to Jerusalem. One was down through Samaria, the way Jesus sometimes came. The other was down the River Jordan valley to Jericho, then up the hills to the west, to Jerusalem. In John, chapter 4, we read that Jesus, going to Galilee, "must needs go through Samaria." Ah, He had in mind to save certain people, hungry-hearted sinners, who were there. And now, no doubt, as He goes for the last time on this trip to Jerusalem, knowing He will die there, He must needs go through Jericho, for He knew of hungry hearts He could save there.

1. Outside Jericho Jesus Healed Blind Bartimaeus

Luke 18 tells of a blind man healed near Jericho as Jesus approached the city. Oh, the word that Jesus healed people had gone out through all the country. People had come from Tyre and Sidon and elsewhere to see Jesus and to have healing. So now you need not be surprised if there were several blind men in the area of Jericho who wanted healing. So Bartimaeus also was healed there.

He heard Jesus passing by and asked who it was, and they told him, "Jesus of Nazareth passeth by." And he cried out for mercy and was wonderfully healed.

Then He went through the city and two other blind men called upon Him to heal them, and He did (Matt. 20).

But Mark tells us that one of these blind men was Bartimaeus, the son of Timaeus.

Here is the story in Mark 10:46-52:

"And they came to Jericho: and as he went out of Jericho with his disciples and a great number of people, blind Bartimaeus, the son of Timaeus, sat by the highway side begging. And when he heard that it was Jesus of Nazareth, he began to cry out, and say, Jesus, thou son of David, have mercy on me. And many charged him that he should hold his peace: but he cried the more a great deal, Thou son of David, have mercy on me. And Jesus stood still, and commanded him to be called. And they call the blind man, saying unto him, Be of good comfort, rise; he calleth thee. And he, casting away his garment, rose, and came to Jesus. And Jesus answered and said unto him, What wilt thou that I should do unto thee? The blind man said unto him, Lord, that I might receive my sight. And Jesus said unto him, Go thy way; thy faith hath made thee whole. And immediately he received his sight, and followed Jesus in the way."

It may well be that when Jesus came out of Jericho, some of that great throng that followed Him told Bartimaeus about the leper healed north of the city as Jesus came in and how he had cried for mercy and Jesus had heard. So now he also calls for healing.

I think probably Mary of Bethany had heard how some time before a fallen woman had wept over the feet of Jesus and kissed His feet and anointed His feet with ointment; so she brought her alabaster box of ointment later to anoint Jesus in the house of Simon of Bethany, after Lazarus was raised from the dead.

One often gets a suggestion from the way another approached Jesus and was blessed.

Bartimaeus was helpless. He was blind, a beggar. There was nothing he could do. His case was hopeless. How like a poor lost sinner that is! A man cannot save himself. A man has no remedy for his wickedness unless God will change his heart. A man has no sense of forgiveness for his sins unless he can rely on Jesus Christ that they are paid for, and trust Christ to forgive them, as He promised. So the healing of Bartimaeus must be an act of mercy, undeserved. There is nothing he can pay. So it is with every poor sinner who comes to Jesus.

Bartimaeus was a beggar. He had on a beggar's garment, I suppose some distinctive dress so people would have pity and give him something. But when he came to Jesus—"he, casting away his garment, rose, and came to Jesus." Ah, he will need that beggar's garment no more! Now he can see. He can work. He can make a living, as do others. Jesus will heal him. And in that faith, when he came to Jesus, Jesus asked, "What wilt thou that I should do unto thee?" And Bartimaeus said, "Lord, that I might receive my sight." Jesus responded, "Go thy way; thy faith hath made thee whole." And "he received his sight, and followed Jesus in the way."

Wonderful Jesus! You walked through Jericho and brought blessing!

2. Jericho Is Where the Publican Zacchaeus Was Saved

It is a charming story in Luke 19:1-10. Let us read it:

"And Jesus entered and passed through Jericho. And, behold, there was a man named Zacchaeus, which was the chief among the publicans, and he was rich. And he sought to see Jesus who he was; and could not for the press, because he was little of stature. And he ran before, and climbed up into a sycomore tree to see him: for he was to pass that way. And when Jesus came to the place, he looked up, and saw him, and said unto him, Zacchaeus, make haste, and come down; for to day I must abide at thy house. And he made haste, and came down, and received him joyfully. And when they saw it, they all murmured, saying, That he was gone to be guest with a man that is a sinner. And Zacchaeus stood, and said unto the Lord; Behold, Lord, the half of my goods I give to the poor; and if I have taken any thing from any man by false accusation, I restore him fourfold. And Jesus said unto him, This day is salvation come to this house, for-

somuch as he also is a son of Abraham. For the Son of man is come to seek and to save that which was lost."

Zacchaeus was a publican, a chief of the publicans. ". . . and he was rich." Publicans were tax collectors. Romans had a strange way of farming out the taxes. A certain area would be given to a man to collect the taxes from that area. He must provide so much. He could assess the taxes himself according to what he thought the people could bear, and he could collect, and all proceeds above what he had agreed to pay the government, he kept for himself. So, the tax collectors or publicans were practically always extortioners. They took all the money they could get. They were always hated. They were counted crooks, and we suppose they usually were.

But Zacchaeus had heard, we suppose, about the conversion of Matthew the publican in Capernaum, who was now one of Christ's disciples, a preacher. At any rate, his heart burned and he wanted to see Jesus.

But there was a problem: he was a short man. At least a thousand people, we suppose, crowded around Jesus, and Zacchaeus could not get near. What will he do?

But he was a wise man, a schemer, and he had an idea. He would run ahead and climb a tree on the route Jesus would walk toward Jerusalem, then he would get a good look at the Saviour! So he did. He climbed a sycamore tree to look over the path.

The guide pointed out a sycamore tree to us as the one Zacchaeus climbed. Certainly that sycamore tree was not 1900 years old. It was not the same tree, but they wanted to impress tourists.

Zacchaeus climbed up that tree and Jesus came along. Oh, knowing the hungry heart of Zacchaeus, He looked up and said, "Zacchaeus, make haste, and come down; for to day I must abide at thy house." Ah, Jesus was going home with him for dinner. So Zacchaeus slid down the tree and was converted before he hit the ground!

He immediately began to tell of his repentance. He said if he had taken anything by false accusation he would restore it fourfold, according to the Jewish law, and of all this riches he had, he would give half of it to the poor!

And Jesus said, "This day is salvation come to this house, forsomuch as he also is a son of Abraham." Yes, not only a son of Abraham by literal descendants but he joined those of us who by faith are children of Abraham spiritually.

Of course, there was a good deal of complaint among the Pharisees and others, but Jesus answered, "For the Son of man is come to seek and to save that which was lost." Oh, the one thing dearest to the heart of Jesus is to save souls.

Now He will go up that steep way to Jerusalem. In the twenty-two miles or so He will be walking up hill, from 1,200 feet below sea level to 2,500 feet above; He goes urgently, for He is looking toward the cross. He will have the triumphal entry. He will weep over Jerusalem. They will find an Upper Room for preliminary meals of the passover season. And there He will wash the disciples' feet, will give them the ordinance of the Lord's Supper. There He will teach them the marvelous sayings in John 14, 15 and 16. There He will have the high priestly prayer and will go to the Garden of Gethsemane to pray. There, after a time, will come Judas Iscariot and the officers and servants of the high priest to arrest Him.

He will be taken and abused and slandered and convicted through the Sanhedrin, then taken to Pilate's judgment hall the next morning, and then be nailed to a cross and die. On this last trip up to Jerusalem, Jesus has so great a burden on His heart that He must die for sinners, and He said, "But I have a baptism to be baptized with; and how am I straitened till it be accomplished!"

But isn't it wonderful that by every roadside He saw the seeking heart and stopped to heal or bless or forgive? That is not strange. Although He might have wept for Himself, He wept for Jerusalem. Although He might have been thinking about His own troubles, in that Upper Room, "Having loved his own . . . he loved them unto the end." He stopped to love them, to teach them, to give them the Last Supper and the last teaching. Jesus, on the cross, prayed for sinners: "Father, forgive them." There

He thought about His mother and provided for her. Then Jesus stopped dying long enough to save the thief on the cross!

Oh, Jericho, what blessing you had! The Lord Jesus has walked through these streets!

X. Christ's Agony in Gethsemane; There Betrayed

The Garden of Gethsemane is not large now. It is on the western slope of the Mount of Olives, facing the city of Jerusalem, across the little brook Kidron. There are now eight very ancient olive trees. Some say they remain from the time of Christ. We doubt that, but they may have sprung from the roots of trees cut down then. At any rate, they are very, very old.

The Garden of Gethsemane was one time much larger than it is now. Part of the garden is taken up by the Franciscan Church of All Nations. It is built over "the Rock of the Agony" where, tradition says, Jesus knelt to pray in the Garden of Gethsemane, though the account in the Gospels does not say He knelt on a rock. At any rate, this was formerly a part of the Garden of Gethsemane.

It has been a great joy to go to the Garden of Gethsemane. A few years ago they would allow us to kneel under the olive trees, each one having his time of private devotions and prayer and praise. But now, tourists have crowded the place, and to keep them from picking the flowers or breaking little bits from the olive trees, they are kept behind a fence and can only look on the garden.

Matthew 26:36-38 tells us that after the Last Supper, after the warning that Peter would betray Him, after the blessed promises in John, chapters 14, 15, 16, and the high priestly prayer in chapter 17, Jesus came to Gethsemane.

Mount of Olives as seen from Jerusalem wall; Gethsemane at left of church in foreground.

"Then cometh Jesus with them unto a place called Gethsemane, and saith unto the disciples, Sit ye here, while I go and pray yonder. And he took with him Peter and the two sons of Zebedee, and began to be sorrowful and very heavy. Then saith he unto them, My soul is exceeding sorrowful, even unto death: tarry ye here, and watch with me."

Mark 14:32-34 tells us the same thing. Luke 22:39 says Jesus "came out, and went, as he was wont, to the mount of Olives; and his disciples also followed him." So Gethsemane was on the Mount of Olives. And Jesus was accustomed to going there often. John 18:1 tells us that Jesus left the Upper Room, which is in the city of Jerusalem and ". . . he went forth with his disciples over the brook Cedron, where was a garden, into the which he entered, and his disciples." So the Garden of Gethsemane on the slopes of the Mount of Olives was where Jesus went that night He was betrayed.

I. IT WAS THE PLACE WHERE JESUS OFTEN CAME

Luke says, ". . . as he was wont . . ." and we are told in John 18:2 that ". . . Judas . . . knew the place . . . ," so he very confidently offered to lead the soldiers of the high priest to arrest Jesus there, where he knew he could find Him.

It is interesting to read in John 8:1, "Jesus went unto the mount of Olives." It is unfortunate that the chapter heading divides that statement of the last verse in the preceding chapter 7. Read the two verses together and we find that after Jesus had the great discussion in the Temple, "And every man went unto his own house. Jesus went unto the mount of Olives." Others had homes to which they could go, but Jesus had none. It was late and so Jesus went into the Mount of Olives, no doubt, to His accustomed place in the Garden of Gethsemane where He would sleep on the ground.

We remember that when one man offered to follow Jesus and be His disciple, Jesus reminded him, "The foxes have holes, and the birds of the air have nests; but the Son of man hath not where to lay his head" (Matt. 8:20).

No doubt Jesus was often hungry and often slept on the

ground. Once we are told that the disciples were so hungry that they walked through a field, took the raw wheat, rubbed it out in their hands and ate it. No doubt Jesus was hungry, too. We know some good women came from Galilee and ministered to Him, but what they could provide would not be luxury and would be only occasionally enough, we suppose.

Jesus came often out to the Garden of Gethsemane. So we are not surprised that Judas found Him here and brought the mob that arrested Him, took Him away to try Him and condemn Him to death.

II. THE AGONY OF GETHSEMANE

When Jesus went into the Garden of Gethsemane that night before the Passover, He knew He had an appointment with death. He knew He would be arrested, blasphemed, scourged and crucified. And yet He went to face it.

1. Jesus Was About to Die

In Matthew 26:37,38 note the burden of Jesus. He ". . . began to be sorrowful and very heavy. Then saith he unto them, My soul is exceeding sorrowful, even unto death." That means Jesus was literally about to die. Luke 22:44 says, "And being in an agony he prayed more earnestly: and his sweat was as it were great drops of blood falling down to the ground." ". . . sorrowful, even unto death"! Jesus was about to die!

It is good that an angel strengthened Him, as Luke says one did. It is good that Jesus prayed, for if there had been no change in the situation, Jesus, broken with the burden of the sins of the world, with His heart broken and His body worn, would have died there in the garden in the agony He was in.

2. We Can Hardly Imagine the Long Burden of Soul That Jesus Carried for the Sins of the World

In Isaiah 50:7 we are told that Jesus set His face like a flint as He went to the cross.

Jesus had said, "But I have a baptism to be baptized with; and how am I straitened till it be accomplished!" (Luke 12:50). Oh, with what urgency He pressed on toward Jerusalem, toward the cross, to get this matter settled, to pay the awful debt that would save sinners!

When people had threatened that Herod would kill Him, Jesus replied:

". . . Go ye, and tell that fox, Behold, I cast out devils, and I do cures to day and to morrow, and the third day I shall be perfected. Nevertheless I must walk to day, and to morrow, and the day following: for it cannot be that a prophet perish out of Jerusalem."—Luke 13:32,33.

We cannot imagine how the heart of Jesus pressed on with a burden like no mortal being could ever carry, a burden for the sins of the world. He must push on to Jerusalem; He must die; He must pay the debt; He must make the plan of salvation complete.

3. Part of the Burden That Broke His Heart Also Was His Love for Sinners

How He had wept over Jerusalem, as told in Matthew 23:37-39 and Luke 19:41-44 and before that in Luke 13:34! He had yearned over every one of these people as a hen would have gathered her brood under her wings.

In John 13 we are told that although He knew that night He was going out to arrest and blasphemy, then trial and crucifixion, "having loved his own . . . he loved them unto the end." With tender compassion He gave the Last Supper. He washed the disciples' feet. He gave them marvelous teachings in John, chapters 14,15, and 16. Then He prayed for them in John 17. I say, the love of Jesus for all His own, including you and me for whom He prayed in that high priestly prayer—that burden of soul for us whom He loved was part of what broke His heart in the Garden of Gethsemane. He sweat "as it were great drops of blood." He was in an agony. He was about to die.

We ought to remember that Jesus had been under such continual pressure; His long hours, lack of sleep, constant going, the triumphal entry, accusations of the priests, the plaudits of the crowd, the certainty that Peter would deny Him, and the knowledge that Judas was coming to give Him a traitor's kiss

Ancient olive trees in Gethsemane

and betray Him—all these things were on the mind of Jesus. His body was worn. It is not surprising that He would have died there in the Garden of Gethsemane had God not rescued Him.

III. SATAN WOULD HAVE KILLED JESUS THERE

To understand fully the agony of Jesus in Gethsemane, and that His soul was sorrowful unto death and about to die, we must remember that Satan wanted to kill Him ahead of time and thus to invalidate and make void the Gospel.

1. The Saving Gospel Is That Christ Must Die "According to the Scriptures"

First Corinthians 15:3,4 tells us this is the saving Gospel, "how that Christ died for our sins according to the scriptures; And that he was buried, and that he rose again the third day according to the scriptures." Jesus Himself foretold that not "one jot or one tittle shall in no wise pass from the law, till all be fulfilled" (Matt. 5:18). And if Jesus must die "according to the scriptures," then there is a very clear outline of how He must die. First, He must be scourged and His beard plucked out, for Isaiah 50:6 says, "I gave my back to the smiters, and my cheeks to them that plucked off the hair. . . ." He must have nails through His hands and feet because it is foretold, ". . . they pierced my hands and my feet" (Ps. 22:16). It must be fulfilled that ". . .they shall look upon me whom they have pierced. . ." (Zech. 12:10). "Behold . . . every eye shall see him, and they also which pierced him . . ." (Rev. 1:7). He must die on the cross, for "cursed is every one that hangeth on a tree" (Deut. 21:23; Gal. 3:13). If Jesus is to bear our curse, it must be on a cross. He was to be mocked, as Psalm 22:7,8 foretells. He must cry out, "My God, my God, why hast thou forsaken me?" (Ps. 22:1). The soldiers must gamble for His garments, as Psalm 22:18 foretold.

Ah, but remember that He must die at the very time passover lambs were slain. For fifteen hundred years lambs had died on the fourteenth day of Nisan, and Jesus must die tomorrow afternoon at the time when the lambs die or He does not fulfill the

type. Remember that I Corinthians 5:7 says, "Christ our passover is sacrificed for us."

So if the Scriptures should be fulfilled, Jesus cannot die here
in the Garden of Gethsemane or the Gospel will be made of none
effect. The only saving Gospel is that "Christ died for our sins according to the scriptures; And that he was buried, and that he
rose again the third day according to the scriptures."

2. Satan Had Tried Often to Ruin the Plan of Salvation

We are sure that Satan motivated King Herod when he had
every boy baby in Bethlehem two years old and under slain, trying to kill the Saviour.

When Jesus had gone to Nazareth and preached where He had
been brought up, there, filled with the Holy Spirit, He spoke so
boldly to them that they wanted Him to work miracles like He
had done at Capernaum and their anger burned hot against Him
and they rushed Him out of the city to the place now called the
"Hill of Precipitation" on which the city is built, and they intended to throw Him down and crush Him there. But He slipped
away from them. Ah, Satan would like to have killed Jesus and
stop this work of the atoning Saviour.

Again the Pharisees more than once "took up stones . . . to
stone him" but they could not throw the stones. The officers sent
to arrest Him were so dumbfounded and nonplussed, they said,
"Never man spake like this man" (John 7:46). When they would
have taken Jesus to kill Him, He slipped away from them. I am
saying, Satan had often tried to block the plan of salvation by
bringing to nought the ministry of Jesus.

And tomorrow on the cross Satan will inspire these wicked
Pharisees and they will order that the legs of Jesus and the two
criminals must be broken so that the ordeal will be over and they
can be taken down from the cross before sundown when the annual high Sabbath begins, the Sabbath when they eat the passover lamb after dark.

Oh, but if they should break the legs of Jesus, that will ruin all
the Gospel. For of the passover lamb picturing Jesus, it was
plainly said, "Neither shall ye break a bone thereof" (Exod.

12:46). John 19:36 calls attention to that rule. Oh, if they break the bones of Jesus, then He cannot be a Saviour. He must die "according to the scriptures." Satan would have ruined the crucifixion, ruined the death of Christ as far as any saving value were concerned, had he had Him die in His agony and bloody sweat in the Garden of Gethsemane.

IV. JESUS PRAYED IN THE WILL OF GOD

1. Jesus' Prayer Often Misunderstood

It grieves my heart to hear preachers tell about the prayer of Jesus in Gethsemane and how Jesus hated to drink the cup of death and wanted to avoid that. Didn't God have some other way to save sinners? Could not Jesus talk the Father out of pressing Him on to the cross? That is a foolish idea. I can read the Old Testament and I well know God has no other way to save sinners but for Jesus to die. Do you think Jesus did not know that? Do you think there was even a moment of hesitation on Jesus' part to go to the cross? No! He pressed His "face like a flint" going to Jerusalem. He had a "baptism to be baptised with" and how was He "straitened till it be accomplished!" No one made Jesus go to the cross. He gave Himself. It is irreverent to suppose that here in the Garden of Gethsemane, after thirty-three years on earth, Jesus is doubting the plan of the Father, and trying to have some other way.

Someone says, "Oh, but the awfulness of bearing the sins of the world." The simple truth is, Jesus knew that and bore that burden before the world ever began. He was as a "Lamb slain from the foundation of the world" (Rev. 13:8). Jesus was not praying against the will of the Father; He was praying, "Father, I am not praying in My will, but in Thine. I do not have any other plan but the plan You have, Father."

His prayer was that the cup might pass on until the proper time instead of coming to death in the Garden of Gethsemane. He knows He must die tomorrow, not tonight. He must die on the cross, not in Gethsemane. He must fulfill the Scriptures, and not please Satan here. So Jesus prayed in the will of the Father, not against it.

2. Jesus Prayed Through and Was Spared

That is what the Scriptures say about Christ. Hebrews 5:7 says, "Who in the days of his flesh, when he had offered up prayers and supplications with strong crying and tears unto him that was able to save him from death, and was heard in that he feared." Notice this description of the prayers of Jesus: "prayers and supplication." For some hours, we suppose, He prayed there. And He came again and again and again to pray the same prayer.

And Jesus wept while He prayed. It was "with strong crying and tears." That is the third time the Scripture tells us that Jesus wept. Once He wept at the grave of Lazarus, recorded in John 11:35. Once He wept over Jerusalem, we learn in Luke 19:41. And here in the garden He wept and pleaded with God "with strong crying and tears" that the cup Satan was trying to press upon Him now, the cup of death in the garden, the cup of failure of all He had tried to do, might pass away until tomorrow when He would take all that God had planned for Him to take, and bear our sins and pay our debts "according to the scriptures." So Jesus prayed through. I do not wonder that He wanted Peter, James and John to pray with Him. Here was one of the greatest battles this world ever saw, when Jesus faced all the infirmity and trouble of heart that Satan could press upon Him. His body was failing. The blood was dripping from His skin, pressed out of the pores because of the awful pressure and burden of His heart.

We are told that Jesus sweat "as it were great drops of blood." Jesus prayed so hard that He sweated. Oh, that we might pray like Jesus did—for the will of God to be done, pray through and never give up.

So an angel came and strengthened Jesus. If God had not heard His prayer, then He would have died in the garden. But, thank God, the Scripture says that when He prayed with "prayers and supplications with strong crying and tears," He was heard. God answered His prayer. He went on to die in the appointed way, in the will of God as He Himself pleaded.

"Not my will, but thine, be done" is a good prayer for us. And it was a good prayer for Jesus. But if you insinuate that Jesus was fighting His own desire to be free and was trying to surrender Himself to the will of God, then you do Christ great wrong. No, He was praying in the will of God, and was heard.

V. THE EXHAUSTED AND TROUBLED DISCIPLES SLEPT

It is not surprising that the disciples went to sleep in the Garden of Gethsemane. Poor, frail things, they had good reason, we think, to fail.

1. They Were "Sleeping for Sorrow"

Luke 22:45 says, "And when he rose up from prayer, and was come to his disciples, he found them sleeping for sorrow." They had gone through so many emotions they were drained, exhausted. They were heartsick. Jesus was going away. Jesus had said He must die, but they did not know why. They did not understand all about the resurrection. You see, we know how things will turn out, but they then did not know. It seemed too much to expect that Jesus would die and then rise again. Even after He was risen, it was hard for them to believe. Can you imagine the sorrow of their hearts?

2. They Were Exhausted, Pressed Out of Measure

We must remember also that they too had been under great stress. How many long hours they had toiled! They had recently come in from Galilee—the long walk, then up those long miles from Jericho. Now, in this Upper Room, they had spent so many hours. They had a preliminary meal of the passover; they had the Last Supper; they had solemn warnings of Jesus about Peter's denial and Judas' betrayal. They had all the teaching that Jesus was going away. He would send the Holy Spirit, the Comforter. Physically tired, mentally exhausted, it is not surprising they went to sleep.

I must confess that I too have sometimes gone to sleep when I tried to pray. Sometimes our human resources fail and it seems we cannot hold on to God longer in persistent prayer. That means, then, that we ought to get rest when we need it, and we ought to be especially on our guard, for had Peter watched and prayed as he ought, he surely would not have fallen into such temptation as Jesus had warned him of.

Sometimes Christians ought not berate themselves for their weakness and their frailty. There is a tender note here when Jesus, after He had prayed through and seemed assured that God had heard Him, said to the disciples, ". . . Sleep on now, and take your rest" (Mark 14:41). God knows how frail we are. He remembers that we are dust and, "like as a father pitieth his children, so the Lord pitieth them that fear him" (Ps. 103:13).

3. I Think There May Have Been Despair in the Hearts of the Disciples

How could you pray with faith and power if utter despair had entered your soul! What if you think the battle is lost and the Saviour is dying and the great plan for all destroyed! So the disciples, in despair and sorrow, may have failed to pray and had gone to sleep.

Let us be very charitable as the Lord Jesus was, in our thoughts on these who prayed but did not as much as they ought. Oh yes, Peter, if you had prayed like you ought to, you would not have fallen into such temptation, for, "the spirit indeed is willing, but the flesh is weak" (Matt. 26:41). God understands that and we ought to understand it about ourselves and with others. Oh, but what a privilege to join with Jesus in persistent prayer, to help bear His burden!

Wouldn't it be a good thing if Christians would some way enter into Gethsemane with Jesus, join Him in prayer, join Him in burden for sinners and then be as willing as He to see the will of God done at any cost?

What sweet lessons there are for us in the Garden of Gethsemane! I never go there without deep moving in my heart. But all of us can have that sweet moving of heart as we study the Scriptures about Jesus and Gethsemane.

XI. Follow to House of Caiaphas; Jesus a Prisoner; Peter Denies Christ

On the slope of the hill south of Jerusalem, the original Mount Zion, above the Valley of Kidron, is the Church of the Crowing Cock. It was built in 1931 by the Assumptionist Catholic Fathers, on a site long accepted as the ruins of the house of Caiaphas, the high priest in the time of Christ. We think it was here where Jesus was taken after His arrest in the Garden of Gethsemane, where the chief priests and scribes assembled to try Him and vote for His death. We think it was here that Peter sat by the fire on the lower floor, next to the soldiers, and denied the Saviour. Let us consider what happened that fateful night.

I. THE PROCESSION FROM GETHSEMANE TO THE PALACE OF THE HIGH PRIEST

Matthew 26:57,58 says:

"And they that had laid hold on Jesus led him away to Caiaphas the high priest, where the scribes and the elders were assembled. But Peter followed him afar off unto the high priest's palace, and went in, and sat with the servants, to see the end."

1. It Was a Subdued Crowd

That is a subdued group, we think, as they left the Garden of Gethsemane, walked down across the Valley of Kidron up to the high priest's house. Jesus is bound, we suppose with His hands tied behind Him. He is surrounded with soldiers carrying swords, spears and clubs. Some of those officers of the high priest and that rabble of servants may have a sense of triumph now that they have arrested Jesus. They wanted so long to kill Him! Now they have Him.

But the more sensible among them must realize they have Jesus only because He was willing to come. For when Judas, who betrayed Him, and the others stood there accosting Jesus, He said, "Whom seek ye? They answered him, Jesus of Nazareth . . . As soon then as he had said unto them, I am he, they went backward, and fell to the ground. Then asked he them again, Whom seek ye? And they said, Jesus of Nazareth. Jesus answered, I have told you that I am he: if therefore ye seek me, let these go their way" (John 18:4-8). And they did. They found they could not even touch Jesus until He gave His permission. Now the sensible among them know Jesus could break those bonds and go anywhere He wished. That mighty power that had cast them backwards could deliver Jesus if He wanted to be delivered.

And wonder fills the face of one man as he goes along in the dark and feels again of his ear. It is there! Peter's sword had slashed at him and cut off his ear. We suppose it hung by a shred. But Jesus had kindly touched his ear, and now it is whole! Then I suppose that servant of the high priest thought, "What are we doing arresting a Man of God like that!" The man felt of his ear again. It was not even sore!

2. Judas Iscariot Was With This Crowd Arresting Jesus

We think Judas is with that crowd going back to the house of Caiaphas. He must receive the thirty pieces of silver promised him for the betrayal of Jesus!

But now Judas is having second thoughts. It may be he will stand about or sit with the servants in the lower floor while the elders accuse and abuse Jesus. And at first daybreak all the Sanhedrin together condemn Him.

But will Jesus actually die? Yes, that is the plan of the scribes and elders of the Jews. They will take Him to Pontius Pilate for sentence.

Stones of steps to present-day "House of Caiaphas."

And we read:

"Then Judas, which had betrayed him, when he saw that he was condemned, repented himself, and brought again the thirty pieces of silver to the chief priests and elders, Saying, I have sinned in that I have betrayed the innocent blood. And they said, What is that to us? see thou to that. And he cast down the pieces of silver in the temple, and departed, and went and hanged himself. And the chief priests took the silver pieces, and said, It is not lawful for to put them into the treasury, because it is the price of blood. And they took counsel, and bought with them the potter's field, to bury strangers in. Wherefore that field was called, The field of blood, unto this day. Then was fulfilled that which was spoken by Jeremy the prophet, saying, And they took the thirty pieces of silver, the price of him that was valued, whom they of the children of Israel did value; And gave them for the potter's field, as the Lord appointed me."—Matt. 27:3-10.

Judas said to the chief priests, "Let us trade back. I don't want this money! Turn Jesus loose!" He cries out, "I have betrayed the innocent blood!" Yes, the only innocent blood this world ever saw this side the Garden of Eden has been betrayed, Judas, and you did it! There is a torment in his soul. Even a lost man, a depraved man who has been led of the Devil, has a conscience, and Judas' conscience was burning like fire. But the chief priests and scribes refused to release Jesus. They say to Judas, "See thou to that!"

So it ever is when those who lead a man on to sin and see him come to ruin—they have no remedy for his heartbreak and ruin. Those who sell the liquor or dope that leads a man to poverty, disgrace and crime, or broken homes, or enslavement, have no remedy then for the drunkard, the fallen man. He must go to some rescue mission, or to some godly preacher to get the help that those who led him to his ruin will not give him.

As I said this while preaching in a revival campaign in a country church near Decatur, Texas, a strange wave of emotion went through the congregation. A young woman began to weep. A number were greatly agitated.

When the service was over and after some had been saved, I was alone with the pastor. I asked him, "Did you notice the agitation of the congregation when I mentioned that Judas, in his sin, would have no sympathy or help from those who had paid him to betray Jesus?" And I said it is ever that way—those who lead into sin then have no remedy for the sinner and no sympathy for his heartbreak.

He told me a story. The young woman I saw weeping had, two Sundays before, come before the church to confess that she had been guilty of fornication and was to have an illegitimate baby. She asked their forgiveness and their mercy, which the church promised. But it was known that the young man who had led this girl to ruin had already gone to another community and had gotten another young woman pregnant. How the thought moved them, that those who lead you into sin have no sympathy, no remedy for you when sin leads to ruin!

So Judas went and hanged himself. The body hung and swung until the rope broke, and falling, his body burst open. I think he had sinned unpardonably. I do not mean that God could not forgive him, nor that God's offer of mercy to any poor sinner was not still held open for him. But he had so sinned against light, had so wickedly rejected every opportunity, that now he was set in character and found no place of repentance. He could not turn his wicked heart to repent.

It is always so about the unpardonable sin. It doesn't change God; it just changes the sinner so he cannot and will never accept the mercy of God. And what a terrible thing that is!

Judas had heard every message Jesus taught, had seen nearly every miracle Jesus did, had felt the lovingkindness of this Son of man and Son of God. He had gone intentionally into his rebellion. He became covetous and a thief. And there had been a hardening of his character so that now he could not turn, yet not live with himself, so he committed suicide.

> There is a time, I know not when,
>   A place, I know not where,
> Which marks the destiny of men
>   To Heaven or despair.
>
> There is a line by us not seen,
>   Which crosses every path;
> The hidden boundary between
>   God's patience and His wrath.
>
> To cross that limit is to die,
>   To die, as if by stealth.
> It may not pale the beaming eye,
>   Nor quench the glowing health.
>
> The conscience may be still at ease,
>   The spirit light and gay.
> That which is pleasing still may please
>   And care be thrust away.
>
> But on that forehead God hath set
>   Indelibly a mark,
> By man unseen, for man as yet
>   Is blind and in the dark.
>
> And still the doomed man's path below
>   May bloom like Eden bloomed.
> He did not, does not, will not know,
>   Nor feel that he is doomed.
>
> He feels, he sees that all is well,

In the Church of the Cock Crowing over the ruins of the high priest's house

His every fear is calmed.
He lives, he dies, he wakes in Hell,
Not only doomed, but damned.

Oh, where is that mysterious bourn,
By which each path is crossed,
Beyond which God Himself hath sworn
That he who goes is lost?

How long may man go on in sin,
How long will God forbear?
Where does hope end, and where begin
The confines of despair?

One answer from those skies is sent,
"Ye who from God depart,
While it is called today, repent,
And harden not your heart."

Oh, Judas and the crowd around the arrested Saviour, what ruin your own sin has brought to you!

3. Peter and John Followed That Crowd to the House of the High Priest

John 18:15,16 tells us:

"And Simon Peter followed Jesus, and so did another disciple: that disciple was known unto the high priest, and went in with Jesus into the palace of the high priest. But Peter stood at the door without. Then went out that other disciple, which was known unto the high priest, and spake unto her that kept the door, and brought in Peter."

John was known to the high priest and to his servants, but Peter was not, so they would not let him in until John came and vouched for Peter.

Peter denied he was a disciple of Jesus, so Peter stood with the servants and officers around the fire on the basement floor and warmed himself. But John may have gone upstairs with the elders and others where Jesus was tried. At any rate, Peter sat with the crowd of enemies because he denied being a disciple of Jesus.

One young man was in the garden when Jesus was arrested. He had a linen cloth about his naked body. The young servants of the high priest seized him but he slipped away. He left the cloth in their hands and ran away in the night naked. Joseph too had left his garment in the house of Potiphar's wife when she tried to seduce him.

Mark is the one who tells us about that young man: "And there followed him a certain young man, having a linen cloth cast about his naked body; and the young men laid hold on him: And he left the linen cloth, and fled from them naked" (Mark 14:51,52). We suppose it was Mark himself, who later wrote the Gospel of Mark. He was the son of Mary and the nephew of Barnabas.

Now the crowd is gone to the house of the high priest. Many of the chief priests and scribes are assembled there waiting for Him. They cannot call an official meeting of the Sanhedrin, we suppose, till daylight, but they mock Jesus and abuse Him.

II. WHY MANY THINK THIS WAS THE SITE OF THE HOUSE OF THE HIGH PRIEST

The present church here was built in 1931.

> "The Irish Archaeologist, Father Power S. J., resumed the entire controversy about the authenticity of this sanctuary and concluded: 'Consequently we have all the rights to believe that the Church of St. Peter in Gallicantu possesses two important evangelical souvenirs: Our Lord's imprisonment, Peter's denial and repentance. Most probably we may add the Apostles' imprisonment and scourging (Acts V, 17).

> "The ruins of the house of Caiaphas were seen in 333 A.D. by the Pilgrim of Bordeaux: 'In the same valley of Siloam, You go up to Mount Sion and You see the spot where the house of Caiaphas stood.' "

Theodosius, in 530 A.D., said, "Straight to the east of the Cenacle you go to the house of Caiaphas, where St. Peter denied the Lord." The great Basilica there of ancient times was destroyed in the fourteenth century, replaced in 1931.

1. Certain Artifacts Were Found Here Which Made It Appear to Be the Ruins of the House of Caiaphas

A huge door lintel of stone was found with the words, "Le asham houa qorban—For the 'sins-asham' is this the qorban," that is, the "depository of the fines for shortcomings in justice." Those fines were imposed besides restitution (Lev. 5:14-16; Ezek. 40:39, etc.). Complete sets of Jewish temple weights and measures were found, such as would be used at the house of the high priest, for the offerings and the penalties exacted of the people. You remember that the Temple had a special money system.

Down in the basement there are cells for a police station and a prison. Some of the square pillars have holes chipped out through a corner so a man's hands could be tied six feet high or so, thus a man could be bound to two pillars for scourging or punishment.

Who besides the Roman officers from the Fortress of Antonia would have authority to arrest, imprison and fine people but the Sanhedrin leaders through the high priest and his house?

2. The Bible Speaks of "the Palace of the High Priest" (Mark 14:54)

This must have been a very extended building, at least three stories, the lower floor with cells and much room for servants. There was a corn mill and store rooms such as would fit a large house with many servants. So we are led to think that this may well be the site of the old house of the high priest where they brought Jesus that night when He was arrested. It was a palace.

III. THE SHAMEFUL ABUSE OF JESUS AT CAIAPHAS' HOUSE

Here they come trooping into the high priest's house. Most of the servants go in on the lower floor and on the pavement have a fire against the cold spring night. Some of the officers take Jesus upstairs to the assembly of priests and elders who have been waiting for Him to come.

1. His Murderous Enemies Were Waiting for Him

We are told that when Christ came to the high priest, "with him were assembled all the chief priests and the elders and the scribes." This is not the official meeting of the Sanhedrin. That will come at daylight. Do you suppose that Joseph of Arimathaea and Nicodemus were here? Probably not. They would not have been in on the plot to pay Judas for betraying the Saviour. They may be summoned tomorrow morning or may not.

But this is the crowd that has been longing to kill Jesus ever since His ministry became very prominent. More than once some had "taken up stones to stone him." More than once they had wanted to kill Him, but He had slipped away. They hated Him all the more when Lazarus was raised from the dead and many, many were taught to believe on Him as the Saviour because of this wonder, this marvel of His power. They even considered killing Lazarus. Now they have Jesus in their hands!

2. They Seek Witnesses Against Jesus to Justify His Death

In Matthew 26:59-61 we learn that they deliberately sought false witnesses:

"Now the chief priests, and elders, and all the council, sought false witness against Jesus, to put him to death; But found none: yea, though many false witnesses came, yet found they none. At the last came two false witnesses, And said, This fellow said, I am able to destroy the temple of God, and to build it in three days."

It is shocking that when people go wrong religiously, they may fall into every kind of sin. Now these who are supposed to be the religious leaders of Israel have deliberately given themselves to covering up the truth, to get false witnesses to condemn Jesus by false testimony, to murder Him!

The truth is there is always a moral guilt in heresy. None of these men were honest in their rejection of Christ as Son of God and Saviour. They turned away from Him as lost sinners do today because they love their sins. As Jesus said in John 3:19-21:

"And this is the condemnation, that light is come into the world, and men loved darkness rather than light, because their deeds were evil. For every one that doeth evil hateth the light, neither cometh to the light, lest his deeds should be reproved. But he that doeth truth cometh to the light, that his deeds may be made manifest, that they are wrought in God."

Now they want false witnesses to put Jesus to death.

Caiaphas' house where Peter denied the Lord.

The dungeon where Jesus may have spent the last part of that terrible night. Now underneath the Church of St. Peter-in-Gallicantu.

At last two false witnesses arose. And how flimsy was their testimony. They said Jesus had promised He could destroy the Temple and build it in three days. Of course, the simple truth is that He had spoken concerning His own body that would rise from the dead in three days. He could have destroyed the Temple and restored it. He had set the sun in the galaxies of Heaven and set the planets in their orbits; could He not have raised the Temple? But they pretend that Jesus was thus talking against the Temple and thus against God and the Jewish religion.

The same people will bring lying accusations against Jesus before Pilate, saying, "We found this fellow perverting the nation, and forbidding to give tribute to Caesar, saying that he himself is Christ a King" (Luke 23:2).

To all their questions and charges Jesus answered nothing. Later before Pilate and Herod He will also refuse to answer, will not defend Himself. He could have done so.

We remember how, when the Pharisees were assembled with the woman taken in adultery and demanded she be stoned, Jesus faced them after writing on the ground, "He that is without sin among you, let him first cast a stone at her." And they being conscience-smitten slunk away!

We remember that when officers were sent to arrest Him, they were dumbfounded. They seemed powerless. They returned saying, "Never man spake like this man."

And in the garden when that crowd came to arrest Him, when He looked upon them and spoke, they all fell backwards to the ground. Oh, He could have spoken so compellingly they could not but release Him. But He would not. Or, He could have had twelve legions of angels to come to deliver Him. But He would not.

Oh, if the Lord should deliver Himself from the cross, then you and I would go to our eternal doom unforgiven, our sins unatoned for, without hope. No, Jesus deliberately put Himself on the road to the cross. He did not defend Himself.

At last the high priest demanded that Jesus answer on oath. He said:

"I adjure thee by the living God, that thou tell us whether thou

be the Christ, the Son of God. Jesus saith unto him, Thou hast said: nevertheless I say unto you, Hereafter shall ye see the Son of man sitting on the right hand of power, and coming in the clouds of heaven."—Matt. 26:63,64.

Will that same high priest Caiaphas see the Lord Jesus in His second coming? I think the lid of Hell may be raised and every sinner will see Him, for it is foretold that every knee shall bow to Christ and every tongue shall confess that He is Lord to the glory of God the Father, both in Heaven and on earth and under the earth. Oh, yes, everybody in Hell must acknowledge the Lordship of Jesus, though they do not love Him.

And now, that is enough. They will condemn Him to die for "blasphemy," for claiming that He is the Son of God.

3. Jesus Buffeted and Abused

Luke 22:63-65 tells us how they abused Jesus now:

"And the men that held Jesus mocked him, and smote him. And when they had blindfolded him, they struck him on the face, and asked him, Prophesy, who is it that smote thee? And many other things blasphemously spake they against him."

They had been holding on to Jesus as if He were a vicious criminal who might escape or attack someone. His hands are bound. Now these wicked servants of the high priest mocked Him and smote Him. They blindfolded Him and struck Him on the face and asked Him, "Prophesy, who is it that smote thee?" Ah, the hate comes out and the wicked chief priests allow it, no doubt encourage it.

Now for some long time Jesus has been in the house of the chief priest. Peter had denied the Saviour, and then "about the space of one hour after" he denied Him again. So they had been there some time.

IV. PETER DENIES THE SAVIOUR

The church built forty-five years ago over the spot which we think is the ruins of the high priest's house is called St. Peter-in-Gallicantu, meaning the Church of St. Peter of the Crowing Cock. Peter had been solemnly warned by the Saviour, "I tell thee, Peter, the cock shall not crow this day, before that thou shalt thrice deny that thou knowest me." Once at the door, the maid keeping the door asked him, "Are you a disciple?" And he said, "No," he was not.

Then he sat in with the other servants, not with the friends of Jesus. He talked with them and later one of them who was a kinsman of the man whose ear Peter had cut off in Gethsemane recognized him and said, "Surely you are one of the disciples," and he denied again.

A third time they said, "Your speech betrays you; you talk like all these Galileans, you must be His disciple." And that time he cursed and swore and went out.

Then he looked and saw Jesus. It must have been a look of pity the Saviour gave him, not a look of scorn nor of hate. Peter was cut to the heart and went out into the dark to weep bitterly. Oh, yes, and so have I gone more than once, ashamed over my sin.

Peter had been warned, but he had solemnly said, "Though I should die with You, I will never deny You, Lord Jesus," and I am sure he meant it.

There are several things that led to Peter's denial. One is he had the old carnal nature which all of us have. It is easier to do wrong than to do right. "The heart is deceitful above all things, and desperately wicked." "The flesh lusteth against the Spirit, and the Spirit against the flesh." Paul said, "When I would do good, evil is present with me."

Then he had a direct attack of Satan. Satan had demanded the right to try him. Peter didn't have to sin, but he did have to be tried. He could have had deliverance, for the Scripture says, "There hath no temptation taken you but such as is common to man: but God is faithful, who will not suffer you to be tempted above that ye are able; but will with the temptation also make a way to escape, that ye may be able to bear it" (I Cor. 10:13). But it was a direct attack of Satan.

Another reason for Peter's failure was he did not pray when Jesus warned him. Instead he was so self-confident he went to sleep. He felt sure he would never fall into such sin. Oh, how much sin we fall into because we do not pray! As Jesus told

Peter, "Watch and pray, that ye enter not into temptation: the spirit indeed is willing, but the flesh is weak." If he had prayed as he should, he would not have fallen into this sin.

Let us be sympathetic toward Peter because this is such an awful time of testing as few people would ever have.

What are the things that led to Peter's restoration and fellowship?

First, Jesus prayed for him. "I have prayed for thee, that thy faith fail not." The Devil cannot have Peter. No, and he can't take any one of God's children. He may get us to sin, but he cannot get our souls. Jesus prayed for Peter and He has prayed for us as our High Priest.

Then Peter had a new nature, thank God. Something in him made him go out and weep bitterly over his sin. One who is saved has already in his heart turned away from an enjoyment and fellowship with sin. His new heart taught him to sorrow over his sins and to return to the Lord's fellowship.

Then Jesus went after him personally. John 21 tells us how He went out on the Sea of Galilee where Peter and others were fishing and there He showed His mighty power, reminded Peter of his call, called him back into service.

And the Lord used fishes and a rooster, just as He could use a donkey with Balaam, or as He used hornets to drive out the Canaanites, or as He had the stars in their courses that fought against Sisera. I say, He used these things to bring Peter back into fellowship.

Oh, Peter, what a normal man you are! And how all of us ought to be solemnly warned by your falling into sin! But how we ought to be comforted that the Lord loved you still and would not let you go!

V. THE SANHEDRIN MEET TO CONDEMN JESUS

Matthew 27:1,2 tells us,

"When the morning was come, all the chief priests and elders of the people took counsel against Jesus to put him to death: And when they had bound him, they led him away, and delivered him to Pontius Pilate the governor."

It is the early morning. The Scripture says it was "early," and John 19:14 says it was "about the sixth hour," 6:00 in the morning, when Pilate said to the Jews, "Behold your King!" In the spring of the passover season the days would be long. The Sanhedrin had met early, quickly condemned Jesus to death, then took Him to Pilate. Pilate's wife went back to try to sleep after they insisted that he come early to the court. She had in her dreams been greatly distressed about Jesus. But now Jesus comes before Pilate. The Jews have condemned Him but they do not have authority to put anybody to death.

Where was Jesus in that short time between His abuse in the house of the high priest and His going before the Sanhedrin? It may have been midnight when He was arrested, for already in that evening they had had the Last Supper, then the giving of the memorial supper, then the warning to Peter and the warning that Judas would betray Him. Then Jesus had gone through the material in John 14, 15 and 16, and then He prayed the high priestly prayer. Then in the Garden of Gethsemane He had stayed in prayer some long while, while the disciples slept.

Perhaps at midnight He went to the high priest's house. Then perhaps a couple of hours later they condemned Him there. So we would suppose He was probably put in a cell only a couple of hours. I have stood in one of those cells under the ruins of the old house of Caiaphas. No sleep for Jesus this night and no peace for that poor, weary body. Then He goes on trial before Pontius Pilate tomorrow.

XII. With Jesus at Pilate's Judgment Hall

In John 19:13 we are told, "When Pilate therefore heard that saying, he brought Jesus forth, and sat down in the judgment seat in a place that is called the Pavement, but in the Hebrew, Gabbatha." After Jesus was brought from the house of the high priest and the trial by the Sanhedrin, He was led across town to the Fortress of Antonia and to Pilate's Judgment Hall and was tried in the Judgment Hall or the Praetorium, or "the Pavement," it is called here.

Now we enter a convent in Jerusalem, on the site of the famous Fortress of Antonia. Here a sister takes us through what is now the basement of the new buildings and shows us "the Pavement" and tells us the story of the trial of Jesus.

I. WHAT EVIDENCES ARE THERE THAT THIS IS THE ORIGINAL PAVEMENT OF PILATE'S JUDGMENT HALL?

We know that many of the traditions about holy places are not reliable. We know that the Angel Gabriel appeared to the virgin Mary somewhere in Nazareth and announced that she would bear the Saviour. But we do not know just where it was, and there is no evidence that the cave which the church of the Annunciation celebrates was the place at all.

We know that Jesus was born in Bethlehem, and the Scripture tells us the Babe was laid in a manger when He was born because there was no room in the inn. But we have no evidence that the cave over which the Church of the Nativity is built now was really the birthplace of Jesus.

We know that Jesus prayed in the Garden of Gethsemane and that there He was betrayed with a kiss, arrested and carried away to Pilate's Judgment Hall. But we do not know just where in the Garden of Gethsemane. Was it on the "Rock of Agony" over which the Church of All Nations is built? We do not know. The Bible doesn't say it was on a rock.

Jesus ascended to Heaven from the Mount of Olives. He went out as far as Bethany and blessed the disciples, then ascended to Heaven. But was that on the site of the little Chapel of the Ascension now? There is no way to know just where it was.

We believe that Gordon's Calvary and the Garden Tomb are authentic, and we do not believe that the Church of the Holy Sepulchre (inside the walls) covers those sites of Christ's crucifixion, burial and resurrection. But God seems to have purposely left it not surely decided in order to discourage people from worshiping places.

Consider the evidence about this place, "The PAVEMENT": is it the place of the trial before Pilate?

1. It Is in the Right Area

We know that the Fortress of Antonia was north of the site of Solomon's Temple and about this very place. There seems no doubt this is where such a pavement ought to be, if it remains.

Not only so, but there are here ruts made by chariot wheels where chariots regularly followed a certain course and the stones are chipped to give purchase to the horses' feet so they would not slip. No doubt chariots regularly went through this pavement, this courtyard.

And there are marks on the great stones, scratched outlines or patterns for games that the soldiers played and over which they gambled. It is not likely that anywhere else there would be soldiers playing such games regularly on permanently marked stones, not likely there would be another place where the Roman army chariots went regularly but at the Fortress of Antonia.

The "Pavement" of John 19:13, of Pilate's judgment hall.

2. This Was at Ground Level

It is below ground level now, after the added dust and debris of centuries and the city destroyed and rebuilt several times. But it was at ground level, and there is no reason why those who tore down the city in A.D. 70 or in 135 A.D. would have taken time to dig out these giant blocks of stone and this paving. It would add to the confusion and there would be no special profit in it.

For the Temple we are told that not one stone would be left upon another. But the west wall of the platform is still there. And we have no reason to believe that this pavement, the ground floor of the great Fortress of Antonia, built with giant blocks of stone so carefully fitted and so greatly used at that day, would have been destroyed. We think it very likely that here we have the remains of that pavement of Pilate's Judgment Hall where the Roman soldiers gathered, where they abused Jesus and led Him away to crucify Him.

II. THE JEWISH ELDERS AND LEADERS
AT THIS PAVEMENT

Yes, they were there. How their hate had burned against Jesus! Now they are here to see Him condemned by Pilate.

1. They Have Already Had Jesus Tried and Condemned to Death by the Jewish Sanhedrin

Christ was taken first to Caiaphas the high priest and there abused and charged. There they tried to get false witnesses against Him. There they put Him on oath as to whether He was the Christ, and under oath He admitted He was. Then about daybreak they had called the elders of the Sanhedrin together and they had voted that Jesus was guilty of death because He blasphemed, because He claimed to be the Son of God, because He claimed that God was His Father, and because He claimed all the attributes of God. They had voted on that.

We learn that Joseph of Arimathaea had not had part in this vote, though he was a member of the Sanhedrin. He was secretly a saved disciple.

Then they had brought Jesus across the city to this Fortress of Antonia. They insisted it be early. Evidently Pilate was rousted out of bed, for Jesus is before Pilate before six o'clock in the morning, before "the sixth hour."

These Pharisees and religious priests would not come into the Judgment Hall lest they be defiled. Oh, how religious they were! But it did not keep them from paying Judas thirty pieces of silver to betray Jesus. Their religion did not keep them from seeking false witnesses to lie about Jesus and get Him condemned. Here before Pilate they prefer a murderer to be turned loose instead of Jesus. How wicked they are!

When Jesus is on the cross, these very religious Pharisees and Jewish priests and elders will insist, "Hurry and break the legs of these men before sundown and get them down. Tomorrow is an high day, the annual passover Sabbath day, and we must not defile that Sabbath day." How strange that they would have such religious convictions that had no morality, no righteousness of heart in them!

Then when Jesus is buried, the tomb is sealed, and then Jesus rises from the dead. In Matthew 28 we find that they will pay large sums of money to the soldiers, bribing them to say, "His disciples came by night, and stole him away while we slept." These conscienceless, wicked people would murder Jesus, yet they are very religious according to the ceremonial law. It is strange that they had the form without the substance, the form of godliness without the power of godliness. How often that is true!

2. They Would Not Be Pacified!

Pilate, wise and, we suppose, ordinarily a just man, said plainly, "I find no fault in him." He did not take seriously their foolish argument that Jesus claimed to be King of the Jews and therefore would be a menace to the reign of Caesar. Of course, he knew that was not true. Jesus had said, "My kingdom is not of this world," this present world system. Pilate insisted that Jesus should be released, but they would not agree to that.

Then Pilate sent Him to Herod and Herod likewise sent back word that he would have nothing to do with this matter. And when Pilate scourged Jesus, that did not satisfy them. They wanted Him crucified. And they chose to have Barabbas, a murderer, released at the passover time instead of Jesus. They would not take any appeasement; they must have Jesus crucified.

III. LET US TAKE A LOOK AT CHRIST AT THE PAVE-MENT OF JUDGMENT

Dear Saviour, forlorn, abused and persecuted, He appears as He comes before Pilate.

1. We Suppose No Man Had Ever Gone Through Such Trouble as Jesus

In the first place, for weeks He had been pressing on toward Jerusalem, facing this crucifixion. After a heavy day of teaching, He had taken time to have the Last Supper, to warn Peter about his coming denial, to warn them that Judas would betray Him.

Then He had taught them in the 14th, 15th and 16th chapters of John. Then with them He had stopped to have the high priestly prayer in John 17. Then He returned to Gethsemane and there— we do not know for how long—for some time He prayed. Weary? All the disciples went to sleep—even Peter, James and John. But Jesus prayed. He prayed in such agony that His sweat was like great drops of blood pressing from His capillaries.

The truth is, He said, "My soul is exceeding sorrowful, even unto death." He was about to die. He prayed "with strong crying and tears unto him that was able to save him from death, and was heard," we learn from Hebrews 5:7. And the angel came and strengthened Him and Jesus had the cup passed over from that night when Satan would have killed Him on till tomorrow, the proper time, when the Scriptures would be fulfilled and He would die on the cross. Oh, how Jesus had been worn! He may have been arrested at midnight or 1:00 a.m. The inquisition at Caiaphas' house may have lasted two or three hours. So Jesus could not have had much rest in the prison cell at the high priest's house before taken at daylight on trial before the Sanhedrin and then before Pilate.

On the cross, Jesus thought, as we learn from the 22nd Psalm, "I may tell all my bones." I would suppose that He had been so emaciated, had lost weight, and His poor, bony, naked body on the cross showed all His bones.

And the Roman scourging often killed people. I can imagine a great lot of blood ran down His back, and the pain was more than we can imagine! And they abused Him, plucked out His beard, crowned Him with thorns. They blindfolded Him, then smote Him with a reed and said, "Prophesy unto us, thou Christ. Who is he that smote thee?" And His face was more marred than any man, says the Old Testament prophecy in Isaiah 52:14.

We need not be surprised now if the Lord Jesus, so worn with no sleep last night, with abuse and beatings and burden and heartbreak and tears, now could hardly carry His cross and they must force Simon of Cyrene to come and carry the cross for Him to Calvary.

2. But Jesus Would Not Defend Himself

We remember that before the high priest He would make no claims until the high priest put Him on oath and said, "I adjure thee by the living God, that thou tell us whether thou be the Christ, the Son of God," then He admitted that He was the Christ. But before Pilate He would make no answer, no defense. Before Herod He would make no defense, would show no miracles. The Lord Jesus, when He was approached in the garden, had such power that the soldiers and servants of the high priest fell backward to the ground and could not face Him. That same power He could have used here. He did not. Oh, He of whom it was said, "Never man spake like this man," so that once before when the priests had sent officers to arrest Him and they could not—He could so speak now that no one would dare accuse Him, no one would dare have Him crucified. But He did not! Remember He gave Himself. He laid down His life and no man took it from Him. It was His choice.

3. Jesus Is Steadfast: "Jesus Christ the Same Yesterday, and To Day, and for Ever"

We can remember that back in Isaiah 50:7 it was prophesied of Him, "Therefore have I set my face like a flint." We remember that Jesus had said, looking forward to the crucifixion, "I have a baptism to be baptized with; and how am I straitened till it be accomplished!"

So wonderful and amazing it is that Jesus carried on with all His faculties until the very hour He gave up the ghost. Having loved His own, He loved them that night and taught them in the Upper Room and washed their feet. In the Garden of Gethsemane when arrested, He said, "Then let these go if you have come for Me." And the rest of the disciples were released and fled.

We remember that on the cross He prayed, "Father, forgive them; for they know not what they do." In the agony of crucifixion, Jesus had still on His heart the one unchangeable burden to keep people out of Hell, to get people saved; and so He prayed for those who murdered Him and condemned Him and mocked Him while He died.

On the cross He remembered His mother and gave her into the care of John. On the cross He stopped dying long enough to save the poor dying thief. Oh, thank God for the unchanging Saviour! We can be sure that He who in the agony of trial, abuse and crucifixion carried His love and His burden, will always do the same for us.

So, dear Lord Jesus, we love Thee as we see Thee on Pilate's Pavement at the Judgment Hall. Our dear Saviour—always the same.

IV. PILATE IN HIS JUDGMENT HALL

Pilate is a prominent figure here at the trial of Jesus. Some have said that it is more like Pilate on trial before Jesus. But Pilate, the Roman governor, had the power of life and death.

1. Pilate Was Carried Along in the Plan of God

We know that Pilate was guilty in his compromise. It is still true that "Surely the wrath of man shall praise thee" (Ps. 76:10). He also makes the folly and the compromises of men to praise Him.

We may be sure that all the details of the crucifixion time had been planned long ago, for Christ was "the Lamb slain from the foundation of the world" (Rev. 13:8). So we cannot think that any of the details of this august and dreadful day were left to an accident or without some supervision by the hand of God.

These things are done "by the determinate counsel and foreknowledge of God," Peter said in Acts 2:23. Now must be fulfilled the prophecy of the 2nd Psalm that the kings of the earth and rulers took counsel against Christ. So it must be true that this crucifixion is officially the plan of the Jewish leaders. It had the approval of Pilate and of Herod. The nations of this world are against Christ and so symbolically it will be carried out. I am saying, Pilate is carried along at this great judgment on the Pavement by the course of history foreordained and planned of God.

I think we can be sure this is why Pilate asked the question, "What shall I do then with Jesus which is called Christ?" I do not think Pilate was a Christian, but I think that is an inspired question. God put it in his heart. God insisted then that Matthew write it down in Matthew 27:22. God wanted every preacher to preach on it and every lost sinner to face it—What must I do with Jesus?

Again it is quite clear that God had a plan in having Pilate make the offer that they could have released Barabbas or Jesus. Which would they choose? They could have a murderer granted to them, or they could have the blameless Son of God! It is God or the Devil; it is Heaven or Hell; it is right or wrong.

And how clear is the choice that men must make and those who turn down Christ take the part of all the wicked and all the sinful in this world and go to the place prepared for those, too.

Pilate was in the stream of history which he could not control.

2. Pilate Was in an Awful Dilemma

He knew that Christ was innocent. He said so. Then when they told him that Jesus claimed to be God, Pilate was concerned even more. Then Pilate's wife sent unto him saying, "Have thou nothing to do with that just man: for I have suffered many things this day in a dream because of him." Evidently when Pilate had left so early in the morning she had tried to sleep and had fretful dreams about Jesus. And it was an added warning to Pilate.

But these rebellious Jews insist on crucifying Jesus. What will he do? We may know that the Jews were a constant threat and some forty years later the Zealots will lead in a great rebellion that will finally mean that General Titus will surround and besiege Jerusalem, it will finally fall and with an awful destruction the city and area will be destroyed, hundreds and thousands of Jews will be killed, and at least fifty thousand will be sold into slavery. It is said that at that later time every tree within miles of Jerusalem was cut down to make a cross on which to crucify a Jew.

I am saying, Pilate had a rebellious populace to consider. What would the emperor want him to do? How could he best control this province that was put under his care? He was in a serious dilemma, and perhaps his job was at stake.

3. But Pilate Gave Up to the Pressure and Compromise

All right, though he plainly told the people it was wrong, he washed his hands. He scourged Jesus, as they insisted, then he turned Him over to the mob of soldiers and to the crown of thorns and the plucking out of His beard, the spittle in His face and mockery, and then he turned Him over to go up the Way of Sorrows, the Via Dolorosa, to Calvary.

Yes, Pilate was carried along in history, but he did not have to do wrong. He could have done right. At least, he may not have been able to release Jesus, but he could have insisted upon it, even if the Jews had seized Him and taken Him to crucify Him against Pilate's will. Pilate compromised and I fear he lost his soul.

V. HOW IT ENDED FOR THOSE WHO MET THAT DAY ON THAT FATAL PAVEMENT

Oh, that Judgment Hall of Pilate! How will it end?

1. Consider How It Will End for This Palace Itself

It will be destroyed. Jerusalem will fall in a great rebellion and then destroyed by Titus and the Roman armies in A.D. 70 and there will be left here only this bare pavement and the mighty palace, the fortress, will be gone.

2. What Happened to Pilate?

Pilate was procurator in Judaea for about ten years. Then because of severity in treatment of his subjects, he was dismissed and went to Rome to face charges.

There are many traditions about him. One is that he committed suicide. Another is that he retired to Switzerland, near Lake Geneva, and that Mount Pilatus there was named for him. The tradition tells that on a moonlit night some have seen two hands rise from Lake Geneva and wash and wash themselves—the hand of Pilate trying to wash away the guilt of sending Jesus to the cross, knowing He was innocent.

Pilate washed his hands, disclaiming any responsibility for the crucifixion. But we know he did not thus free his soul from sin. If he died unsaved, it may be that in Hell he lifts his guilty hands in an agony too late for cleansing from the blood of Christ.

In Shakespeare's "Macbeth," the Macbeth who, with his wife, murdered the king, was hounded by his conscience. With blood on his hands he said,

> "Will all great Neptune's ocean wash this blood
> Clean from my hand? No; this my hand will rather
> The multitudinous seas incarnadine,
> Making the green one red."

And Lady Macbeth, who helped murder the king, cries out, "Out, damned spot! out, I say!" And again she says, "Here's the smell of the blood still: all the perfumes of Arabia will not sweeten this little hand. Oh, oh, oh!"

Let Pilate remind us that there is no cleansing from the awful guilt of sin but by the blood of Christ. And no avoiding the

Outline on pavement of games soldiers played

haunting of conscience and eternal retribution but by trusting Christ!

3. What About These Jews Who Hated Jesus and Led Him to His Death?

Jesus said, "When ye shall see Jerusalem compassed with armies, then know that the desolation thereof is nigh" (Luke 21:20). So we know Jesus had told them. He had wept over Jerusalem and said, "Behold, your house is left unto you desolate" (Luke 13:35). He warned them that they should flee to the mountains for terrible destruction was coming to Jerusalem, and not only these Jews but around the world the curse went with these Christ-rejecting Jews.

Remember they cried out to Pilate that he need not take the blame. "His blood be on us and on our children." So you may be sure that as the sins of the father are put on the children, so children take up the ways of their fathers and suffer as their fathers. So Jews everywhere have suffered because they rejected the Saviour.

I told the story of salvation to a prominent Orthodox Jewish woman on a Santa Fe train to Los Angeles. Her husband ran the largest Kosher market in a province of Canada. Her father was a rabbi. When I said, "I am a better Jew than you are because I have a sacrifice and you have no sacrifice," she asked what I meant; then I told her the story of Jesus. I told the story of His crucifixion, and she stood in the aisle of that pullman car and wept. She said, "Oh, that was wicked! The Jews will sure have to suffer for that!"

I told her that not only the Jews but everybody else who had part in the crucifixion—Pontius Pilate, the Roman governor, Herod and others. And, of course, I told her that we, too, were represented in that crowd that crucified Jesus.

But she was right. The Jews have had to suffer for their part in the crucifixion of Jesus. Those now in Jerusalem who bemoan the six million Jews who were slaughtered by Hitler—do they realize that is because they were rebels against God and rejected the Saviour whom God sent? So it surely is. No one gets by with sin, and the sins of the fathers are visited on the children to the third and fourth generations, and sometimes beyond.

Oh, we want Jews to have a home, but there is just one way for them to have a permanent home on earth or a home in Heaven, and that is to return to Christ with all their hearts in penitence and faith.

4. How Will It End for You?

And now I come to a concluding word. Oh, you who read this today, or some of you who stand with me from time to time in Jerusalem and look on that Pavement where we think Jesus walked, and where Pilate stood in judgment, where the Jews made their raucous cries against Christ and demanded His crucifixion—What will you do with Jesus? You see, every person has to face that. You must decide it.

I have sometimes preached on that wonderful text in Matthew 27:22, and I have asked people to first analyze the question. It is an "I" question. It is a "Jesus" question. It is a "do" question. You have to do something about it, about Jesus. What will you do?

Second, I say it is an unavoidable question. There is no other way to Heaven. The Lord Jesus is not only Creator but He sustains all life. He keeps your heart beating. He keeps the earth in its revolution going around the sun. He puts every breath in your body. You can't dodge Jesus Christ. It is Jesus or Hell.

Third, it is Jesus or Barabbas. To reject Christ is to choose sin. Maybe you want your own way. Maybe some particular sin. Maybe you have followed some awful leading of-Satan. But it is Jesus or Barabbas, God or the Devil, Heaven or Hell for you. Which will you choose?

Fourth, what you do with Jesus will decide what He will do with you. The question now is, What will you do with Jesus? But at the great white throne judgment when the books are opened and every man is to be judged according to his works and those whose names are not written in the book of life will be cast into the lake of fire, then the question will not be, What will you do with Jesus? It is too late for that. The question will be, Jesus, what will You do with these Christ-rejecters, these who chose Barabbas instead of Christ, these who went their way in sin unrepentant and unconverted?

Last of all, I make the proposition, What can you do with Jesus? What are the alternate choices?

1. You can be for Him instead of against Him. Surely that is right.

2. You can love Him instead of hate Him. In Matthew 6:24 Jesus said, "No man can serve two masters: for either he will hate the one, and love the other; or else he will hold to the one, and despise the other. Ye cannot serve God and mammon." Will you love Him or hate Him?

3. You can accept Him or reject Him. The plan is plain. "But as many as received him, to them gave he power to become the sons of God, even to them that believe on his name" (John 1:12). If you receive Jesus, you have everlasting life. He says in Revelation 3:20, "Behold, I stand at the door, and knock: if any man hear my voice, and open the door, I will come in to him, and will sup with him, and he with me." Will you accept Him or reject Him? Will you gladly receive Him or drive Him away with hate and rebellion and procrastination?

And one other word: you can confess Him or deny Him. And He has a wonderful promise in Matthew 10:32, "Whosoever therefore shall confess me before men, him will I confess also before my Father which is in heaven."

In Jesus' name, have you opened your heart's door to Jesus and trusted Him to come in and have you been saved?

One of my songs says:

> Jesus is here, Jesus is here,
> Here on the doorstep He's waiting so near,
> Not far away, but ready today,
> Your poor lost soul this moment to save.

> Whosoe'er will, whosoe'er will,
> May take the water of life to your fill.
> Jesus has paid, His life down He laid,
> For all your sins, atonement He made.

> Don't turn away, don't turn away
> From the soft warning, your conscience would say.
> God's broken laws, your sin and your fall,
> Oh, do not grieve God's Spirit who calls.

> Jesus, come in; Jesus, come in;

Oh, lift the burden, forgive all my sin.
Conquer, O mild One, my heart so wild,
Take now and cleanse and make me God's child.

Open your heart's door to Jesus,
He's standing near, waiting to hear
Your heart's confession and He'll take possession,
So open your heart's door and let Him come in.

XIII. Calvary, Place of a Skull;
the Garden Tomb

"And when they were come to the place, which is called Calvary, there they crucified him, and the malefactors, one on the right hand, and the other on the left."—Luke 23:33.

"This title then read many of the Jews: for the place where Jesus was crucified was nigh to the city: and it was written in Hebrew, and Greek, and Latin."—John 19:20.

In these fourteen annual visits I have made with a group of Christians to the Bible lands, I have preached and taught them the best I could the spiritual and scriptural significance of each place we stopped. Each year we had a time of moving rededication in the Mamertine Prison in Rome where we think Paul wrote his last epistle, Second Timothy, and where he died. We have been refreshed and blessed at the ruins of Capernaum. We reviewed the call of Peter, Andrew, James and John and the wonderful healings there where Jesus made His home, after moving from Nazareth. But the crowning time was always when we gathered at the Garden Tomb, and in our minds went over the blessed truths of the crucifixion, burial and resurrection of our dear Saviour!

The hill we believe is Calvary is now covered by a Moslem cemetery. It is outside Jerusalem on the north. And down below it, nearby, is the garden where we gather. The tomb here is cut in solid rock which we believe was Joseph's tomb where Jesus was buried and from which He arose.

I. SO JESUS WENT TO CALVARY

Let us think for a moment of that sad day, yet that glorious day, when were fulfilled all the promises of an atoning Saviour's death on the cross. Then were fulfilled all the lambs of sacrifice as they had their culmination in the death of the Lamb of God. All human history before and after looks back to this, the highest point in God's dealing with men.

1. Jesus Was Condemned in Pilate's Judgment Hall

In the Fortress of Antonia He had been accused by the hating scribes and chief priests. He had been sent to King Herod there in the palace and then returned to Pilate, after being mocked and crowned with thorns and the scarlet robe put on Him. The crowd had chosen Barabbas to be released and Jesus to be crucified. He was scourged with the Roman cat-o'-nine-tails, then sent forth to bear His cross to Calvary.

It may be that because He was so weak and stumbled, or fainted, that it caused the soldiers to lay hold on Simon, a Cyrenian, compelling him to bear the cross.

They plodded through the streets and then outside the city they climbed this little hill. Women wept alongside them and Jesus told them, "Weep not for me, but weep for yourselves, and for your children."

2. He Was Crucified With Two Criminals

It was written about Jesus: ". . .he was numbered with the transgressors" (Mk. 15:28; Isa. 53:12). So scribes and Pharisees accused Him of blasphemy and wanted Him branded as a sinner. On one side they put one condemned criminal, and on the cross on the other side another criminal, and Jesus, as if He were the greatest criminal, in the center. We suppose they laid Him on the cross and spikes were driven through His hands and then through His feet, and the cross raised up and put in a hole prepared for it.

The crucifixion was about 9:00 in the morning. There He hung while the crowd gathered and mocked Him. We suppose flies gathered on His bloody face where they plucked out the beard, and on His head pierced with thorns, and on His raw and bleeding back cut with the Roman scourge. The blood drained away.

The people urge Him, "Come down from the cross and we will believe on You!" The thief beside Him curses and rails at Him. One thief turns to Him for mercy and is saved. Jesus prays, "Father, forgive them; for they know not what they do."

Over His head Pilate had them write the inscription in Latin, Hebrew and Greek: "JESUS OF NAZARETH THE KING OF THE JEWS." Oh, this crucifixion is on the part of Rome with its Latin language. It represents the Jews with the Hebrew language, and the Gentile world that speaks principally Greek. Christ is dying for the sins of the whole world.

About midday the sun stops shining and the sky is black. Dr. Bob Jones says that the sun looked down and saw her Creator in agony on the cross and in shame hid her face. The rocks looked on their God abused on the cross and their hearts broke and the earth quaked. The darkness went on. Jesus has given His mother into the hands of John for care. At long last He cries out, "It is finished," and with a loud cry He gives up the ghost.

The chief priests and scribes who hated Jesus and so planned His death and paid the traitor's fee, now say, "Let us finish this business. Tonight at sundown starts the annual high Sabbath day when the passover lamb is eaten. These bodies must be down from the cross by sundown. Have the soldiers break their legs. Get this over; get them down."

We suppose the soldier takes his Roman battle-ax and chops at the legs of a thief and breaks the bones, the blood gushes out and a moan or a cry and he is gone. And so with the other thief.

But when he comes to Jesus, behold, He is dead already! He has already finished the atonement and has committed Himself to the keeping of the Father and is gone.

So a soldier, not knowing that he is thus fulfilling the Scripture, runs a spear up into His side and there gushes out blood and water. Ah, now it is true, ". . .and they shall look upon me whom they have pierced" (Zech. 12:10).

3. The Burial of Jesus

We suppose the bodies of those thieves were torn down carelessly from the cross and dumped in the Vale of Hinnom where they threw the garbage. Or, it is possible they were buried in a pauper's field.

But is that what will happen to the body of Jesus? No. Here is a man with a deeply troubled face. He is Joseph of Arimathaea, a rich man. He is a disciple of Jesus and a member of the

Joseph's Garden Tomb where we believe our Lord was buried and arose

Sanhedrin. He did not take part in the condemnation, but perhaps he did not tell anybody that he was a believer in Christ. He was a secret disciple. Now he comes boldly to Pilate and demands the body of Jesus.

Pilate, no doubt, was surprised. He inquires of a soldier, "Has Jesus been some time dead?" Yes; so Pilate will allow them to take down the body of Jesus.

And here is Nicodemus, also a member of the Sanhedrin, the

man who came to Jesus by night and there learned, "Ye must be born again."

Together they gently pull the spikes and lift that poor, abused, bloody body down from the cross. They wrap that naked body and carry it down to the garden below. We believe they laid it on a slab over to my right here, and took water from that cistern in the garden and washed the body.

Oh, the face is swollen where they pulled out His beard, where they beat Him over the head with reeds and said, "Prophesy unto us, thou Christ, Who is he that smote thee?" His body is emaciated. They may "tell all my bones," it was said of Him in Psalm 22:17. How He pressed Himself these days passed, going on to the cross with a holy urgency, then the sufferings of Gethsemane, the bloody sweat, the agony of soul, then the abuse, crucifixion and death. Poor body of the Saviour! The stripes on that back should be on mine. Those wounds in His hands, feet and side ought to be my wounds. I am the sinner who deserved all those things!

Joseph said, "This is my garden. I have cut into the rock here a tomb for myself. I will use it for Jesus. He will be buried in my tomb!" And Nicodemus says, "I will buy the fine linen and the hundred pounds of spices to wrap this body in to keep it from decay and stench as long as we can."

But as they laid the body out, I imagine Joseph has a startled thought: "Wait! His body is longer than mine." They measure; the tomb is too short. So I suppose Joseph sent a servant with a chisel and mallet to chisel out further in the tomb to make it long enough to fit the body of Jesus. We see in the Garden Tomb such an extension made, and doubtless with this reason.

Then they wrap the body in the fine linen with spices "as the manner of the Jews is to bury."

Some women standing by are weeping as they see all that is done.

But the scribes and elders go to Pilate the next day and tell him, "Well, Jesus said He would rise the third day. His disciples may come and steal the body, Pilate, seal the tomb so nobody can take it!" Pilate tells them they have a watch; soldiers guard

Inside the tomb carved out of solid rock

the tomb. It is sealed with the Roman seal. And they go away.

II. IS THIS THE REAL PLACE OF THE CRUCIFIXION AND BURIAL OF JESUS?

We understand that the Church of the Holy Sepulchre is claimed to be the place of the crucifixion and burial of Jesus. Queen Helena, mother of Emperor Constantine, came to Palestine in 324 A.D., and this 80-year-old Christian woman, not well taught, we suppose, but very sincere, selected here a site which she thought was the place of the crucifixion and the burial, and those places are covered with the Church of the Holy Sepulchre. She had a church built there and the Catholic tradition insists that that is the place.

However, some things are against it. In the first place, Queen Helena came nearly 300 years after the crucifixion. Jerusalem had been destroyed utterly in A.D. 70, with not a stone of the Temple left one upon another, and Jews had been killed out and scattered to all the world. In A.D. 135 there had been another

The author examines where Christ's body lay

destruction of Jerusalem, so terrific that it was said that a team of oxen pulled a plow across the face of what was once a city. There is no possibility that anybody was alive who remembered the place, no records but those in the Bible to show where it was. The guess of an old woman, who meant well, is not good evidence that that is the place.

Then the Church of the Holy Sepulchre is within the city, but the Scripture says in John 19:20 of the superscription over the cross, "This title then read many of the Jews: for the place where Jesus was crucified was nigh to the city." And Hebrews 13:12 says that Jesus "suffered without the gate." And we are to go to Him "without the camp."

Our Catholic friends say that the city wall once left that site outside the city, but there is no convincing evidence of it.

Is there evidence that this tomb outside the city is the place, this little hill with the Moslem cemetery on top, the hill called Calvary in the Bible? We think it very probably so.

In 1881 General Gordon, the English General who was a Christian, was in Jerusalem and studied on this matter. Two or three years before a German Christian had suggested that this was probably the hill Calvary. Gordon looked the thing over and saw this place.

1. It Was Outside the City, as Calvary Was Supposed to Be

Recent excavations have been made at the foot of the Damascus gate, on the north side of the city, and there, I am told, they found indications that the original wall of the city was here, as it is today. If so, then the Church of the Holy Sepulchre would not have been outside the wall, but inside, as it is now.

2. This Looks Like the Place of a Skull

On the north side of the city, an excavation cut through the ridge of Mount Moriah, outside the city wall, to make the wall more impregnable. Some think that was done in Solomon's day. Others say it was done by the Maccabees some 400 years B.C. At any rate, it left a jagged side of the hill, and there are holes that seem like the eyes in a skull and a projection looks like the nose.

The Hill of Calvary, "Place of a Skull"

When the light shines a certain way, it looks enough like a skull that the place could have been called "the place of a skull," as it is today.

3. If That Hill Is Calvary, Then There Should Be a Garden Nearby

So General Gordon had people dig and throw out the trash and debris of the centuries at the foot of this hill. They found first a window looking into a grave. It was where the sun could have shone in. They dug down further and found a door and a trough where a great round stone would have been rolled to cover the door. Inside they found a tomb hewn out of solid rock, with room for two or three graves, beautifully carved out of stone. There is evidence that this was a garden. There were cisterns, a wine press, etc. It was near. It fitted the requirements. It seemed to be the place.

4. Calvary Must Be on Mount Moriah

The Bible makes much of Mount Moriah. It was there

Abraham was to go three days' journey from Beer-sheba to offer Isaac on Mount Moriah. Then David bought the threshing floor of Araunah the Jebusite on Mount Moriah. Then Solomon built the Temple there, a place of sacrifice. Remember that Isaac was to be offered as a type of Christ. Remember that the threshing floor of Araunah was bought as a place of sacrifice. The Temple itself had the brazen altar where the sacrifices were offered. Surely if Christ is the Lamb of God that takes away the sin of the world, the One pictured in the Old Testament sacrifices, then He ought to be offered on Moriah.

Mount Moriah is a ridge that goes through the city of Jerusalem. On one end of it is the site of Solomon's Temple, a large platform. It goes on north and comes out at the wall of Jerusalem. And outside a cut was made next to the wall, about a hundred yards wide, and then the highest part of Mount Moriah is what is now called Gordon's Calvary.

The Church of the Holy Sepulchre is not on that ridge. There would be no reason for the types if the Lord Jesus were to be crucified somewhere else; then why should the Lord so

Another view of Gordon's Calvary

meticulously point again and again to Mount Moriah? We think therefore that the hill on which the Moslem cemetery is, above the Garden Tomb, is the original Calvary of the Bible.

5. But Let Us Not Worship Places

However, let us say again, God evidently intended it not to be a settled surety about the place. God does not want people worshiping places. He seems to have deliberately left some shadow, some doubt about all the important places of His birth, ministry, crucifixion, burial and resurrection. There is no doubt about the fact, nor about the general area, but particular places are often not possible to identify.

For instance, He ascended from the Mount of Olives, but where on that mountain? There is no way to tell. People would presumptuously select a place, but they would not know.

Where in Nazareth did the angel appear to Mary? It was in Nazareth, but what spot there we could not possibly know. It was only a guess that made Queen Helena select the cave as place for the Church of the Annunciation there in Nazareth. And so with the cave in Bethlehem where tradition says Jesus was born.

Let us be glad of this: Jesus was born. And He is my Saviour.

Two men were arguing about the place of the crucifixion. One said, "I believe it was at the Church of the Holy Sepulchre." Another said, "I believe it was on this place called Calvary." And one good man said, "I have been to both places; Jesus was not there. He is risen from the dead!"

The fact that I have Christ in my heart and the fact that He does live and is my Saviour, is far more important than the very place of His crucifixion or burial.

But it is a joy to see the place which meets the requirements and thus to remember those details of how my Saviour suffered and died and arose.

III. BUT CHRIST AROSE FROM THE DEAD

The tomb is sealed. Soldiers watch outside. There Jesus lay in the grave "three days and three nights," as He plainly said He would (Matt. 12:40). We believe Jesus was crucified on Wednesday. He was in the grave then Thursday, Friday and Saturday.

Sometime Saturday night He arose from the dead. As Dr. R. A. Torrey said, "He must be in the grave as much as 72 hours; He could be more and fulfill the Scripture but not less and fulfill the Scripture of 'three days and three nights.' "

People have been misled because the day He was crucified a Sabbath began at sundown, but that was not the regular weekly Sabbath for "that sabbath day was an high day" (John 19:31). This was the day of the preparation and at sundown the annual Sabbath of the passover supper would begin. Exodus 12:14-16 tells us of this Sabbath:

"And this day shall be unto you for a memorial; and ye shall keep it a feast to the Lord throughout your generations; ye shall keep it a feast by an ordinance for ever. Seven days shall ye eat unleavened bread; even the first day ye shall put away leaven out of your houses: for whosoever eateth leavened bread from the first day until the seventh day, that soul shall be cut off from Israel. And in the first day there shall be an holy convocation, and in the seventh day there shall be an holy convocation to you; no manner of work shall be done in them, save that which every man must eat, that only may be done of you."

So that high Sabbath would be a day of "holy convocation," and "no manner of work shall be done" on this high Sabbath except that every man should eat. So on this annual Sabbath which came on Thursday Jesus was already in the grave. Then Saturday was the regular weekly Sabbath and that night Jesus arose or before daylight on the first day of the week.

1. Three Sad, Sad Days Went By

I am sure it seemed like the end of the world to the disciples. The good women watched and so they prepared as soon as the weekly Sabbath was gone that they would bring spices to put with the body again. Oh, to keep away decay and stink as long as they could!

And Peter went back to Galilee and to fishing. He thinks he is ruined as a preacher anyhow—who would want to hear an old cussing preacher? Others have gone with him.

Two men go down the road to Emmaus. How sad they are! A

Stranger walks alongside them and says, "What makes you so sad?" They answer, "The things that happened at Jerusalem." And He said, "What things?" And they told Him about the Man Jesus and said, "We hoped He would be the One to redeem Israel." But now He is dead, their hope is gone. Oh, people were sad, they did not yet understand that He would rise from the dead.

2. When the Lord Jesus Arose, They Could Hardly Believe It!

Those two men on the road to Emmaus walked alongside the Stranger. He said to them, "O fools, and slow of heart to believe all that the prophets have spoken: Ought not Christ to have suffered these things, and to enter into his glory? And beginning at Moses and all the prophets, he expounded unto them in all the scriptures the things concerning himself."

They still did not know this was Jesus. They could not believe that. We see what we expect to see; and they did not expect to see Jesus. They stopped some place for something to eat and persuaded Jesus to stay with them for a meal. And, behold, as He broke the bread and blessed it, there was something in the sweet, familiar tones and gestures that they recognized. It was Jesus!

Oh, women had been to the grave and had come reporting that they had seen an angel and he told them that Jesus was alive! But they thought, "You know how hysterical women are. We don't believe that."

When the women had come back from the tomb of Jesus and reported that they had seen an angel, the tomb was empty. The angel said He was risen, "And their words seemed to them as idle tales, and they believed them not," says Luke 24:11.

And when Jesus appeared to the disciples, He showed them His hands and His feet and said, "Behold my hands and my feet, that it is I myself: handle me, and see; for a spirit hath not flesh and bones, as ye see me have. And when he had thus spoken, he shewed them his hands and his feet. And while they yet believed not for joy, and wondered, he said unto them, Have ye here any meat?" So He ate broiled fish and honeycomb before their eyes.

Thomas did not see Him at that time, and when later He came

again Thomas had said, "I will never believe it! I saw Him die! Until I can put my finger in the nailprints of His hands and in the wound in His side, I will never believe it" (John 20:24-29).

So when Jesus came again, He asked Thomas to put his hand in the wound in His side and touch the nailprints and Thomas believed. He cried out joyfully, "My Lord and my God!" How hard it was to convince them that Jesus was alive from the dead! The best evidence that Jesus was actually risen is that all these, against their stubborn unbelief were convinced and had to believe that Jesus was alive from the dead.

3. Jesus Was With Them Forty Days Before His Ascension

After Jesus arose from the dead, He gave commandments to the apostles "to whom also he shewed himself alive after his passion by many infallible proofs, being seen of them forty days, and speaking of the things pertaining to the kingdom of God" (Acts 1:3). Paul gives an inspired account of those who saw Jesus after His resurrection:

"And that he was seen of Cephas, then of the twelve: After that, he was seen of above five hundred brethren at once: of whom the greater part remain unto this present, but some are fallen asleep. After that, he was seen of James; then of all the apostles. And last of all he was seen of me also, as of one born out of due time."—I Cor. 15:5-8.

We know that He appeared to the disciples there in Jerusalem. He appeared to them on a mountain in Galilee where He had appointed them. He appeared to Peter and others as they fished in the Sea of Galilee. And there He called Peter again to come back to the work and "feed my sheep."

And one time a crowd of over five hundred people saw Him at once, and there could be no possible doubt. People saw Jesus. They felt of His body. They saw Him eat and drink. They heard Him speak. The proofs were absolutely "infallible" that Jesus had risen from the dead.

During that time He gave the Great Commission. It is recorded five times as He gave it from time to time during the forty days. Once it is given in Matthew 28:18-20. Again it is given in Mark 16:15,16. And in Luke 24:46-49 Jesus gave it again and told the disciples they must preach the Gospel in all nations but to "tarry. . .in the city of Jerusalem, until ye be endued with power from on high." In John 20:19-22 He breathed on them and said, "Receive ye the Holy Ghost. . .as my Father hath sent me, even so send I you." And in Acts 1:8 He told them, "But ye shall receive power, after that the Holy Ghost is come upon you: and ye shall be witnesses unto me both in Jerusalem, and in all Judaea, and in Samaria, and unto the uttermost part of the earth."

Then one grand day He led them out to Bethany on the back side of the Mount of Olives. He gave them the Great Commission for the last time; then as they beheld He was taken up to Heaven and a cloud received Him out of their sight. And two angels stood by to give the blessed assurance He is coming back! "This same Jesus, which is taken up from you into heaven, shall so come in like manner as ye have seen him go into heaven" (Acts 1:11).

And with great joy the disciples went out to win souls and carry out the Great Commission.

And now the story is told of the Saviour's crucifixion, burial and resurrection here from Joseph's new tomb. Praise the Lord!

He is alive! Oh, yes, He lives within my heart. He is my Saviour.

Coming back? Oh, yes, He is, but the blessed Holy Spirit is within me now, my Comforter, my Guide, my Teacher, my Prayer Helper, sweet manifestation of the Lord Jesus Himself. And one sweet day He is coming back for all of us. Jesus is alive from the dead!

XIV. Mount of Olives Where Jesus Ascended to Heaven

The Mount of Olives is east of the walled city of Jerusalem. Looking way east across Jordan and the Dead Sea from the mountains of Moab and Mount Nebo, one can see the Mount of Olives which is higher than the walled city of old Jerusalem.

The Valley of Kidron is between the city and the Mount of Olives. In that valley are the tombs of the kings, the monument reared by Absalom and traditionally the tombs of Zacharias and James. It is also called the Valley of Jehoshaphat.

In the valley is the Pool of Gihon, where Solomon was crowned King. The Pool of the Virgin is a modern name for it. Further on down the valley is the Pool of Siloam. In Hezekiah's day when the Assyrian Sennacherib came to besiege Jerusalem, King Hezekiah walled up and closed the Pool of Gihon. And he built a tunnel some 1,700 feet through the rock and back to the Pool of Siloam which was then within the walled city. Thus the waters were available to Jerusalem but not to Sennacherib. That tunnel is still there. My brother and some of our tour members took flashlights and waded through that tunnel.

On the north of the Mount of Olives is Mount Scopus where was the old Jewish University. To the left is the small hill called the Mount of Scandal where Solomon built temples for his heathen wives.

Jesus was often on the Mount of Olives.

I. HERE WAS THE HOME OF MARY, MARTHA AND LAZARUS

On the Mount of Olives were two villages, Bethany and Bethphage. Bethany is more or less on the back side of the mountain. Jesus sometimes stayed here. And here Martha was "cumbered about much serving" and here Mary sat at the feet of Jesus and heard Him speak.

1. It Was Here That Jesus Cursed the Barren Fig Tree

In Mark 11:12-14 is the story:

"And on the morrow, when they were come from Bethany, he was hungry: And seeing a fig tree afar off having leaves, he came, if haply he might find any thing thereon: and when he came to it, he found nothing but leaves; for the time of figs was not yet. And Jesus answered and said unto it, No man eat fruit of thee hereafter for ever. And his disciples heard it."

The disciples went on to Jerusalem and returned that night, probably after dark. The story continues in verses 20 to 24:

"And in the morning, as they passed by, they saw the fig tree dried up from the roots. And Peter calling to remembrance saith unto him, Master, behold, the fig tree which thou cursedst is withered away. And Jesus answering saith unto them, Have faith in God. For verily I say unto you, That whosoever shall say unto this mountain, Be thou removed, and be thou cast into the sea; and shall not doubt in his heart, but shall believe that those things which he saith shall come to pass; he shall have whatsoever he saith. Therefore I say unto you, What things soever ye desire, when ye pray, believe that ye receive them, and ye shall have them."

A wonderful promise was made on the Mount of Olives.

2. It Was on the Mount of Olives That Jesus Raised Lazarus From the Dead

In John, chapter 11, we are told how Lazarus was sick. The sisters sent frantically to Jesus, "He whom thou lovest is sick." He intentionally stayed away four days until Lazarus died. Then He came. Martha ran to meet Him and He told her, "Thy brother shall rise again." He sent for Mary and she, too, said as her sister Martha had said, "Lord, if thou hadst been here, my brother had not died." But Jesus wept with the sisters and loved ones; went by the graveside and there called Lazarus forth. He came forth bound hand and foot. And Jesus said, "Loose him, and let him go."

And Jesus loved this home and loved Mary, Martha and Lazarus.

3. It Was Here Where They Had a Marvelous Supper at Bethany, Celebrating the Resurrection of Lazarus

John, chapter 12, tells us more of the story. They had a great supper at the house of Simon the leper in Bethany (Mark 14:3) and Martha was among those who served and Lazarus sat at the table with Jesus. "Then took Mary a pound of ointment of spikenard, very costly, and anointed the feet of Jesus, and wiped his feet with her hair: and the house was filled with the odour of the ointment" (John 12:3). Judas Iscariot and others rebuked her and said that this very expensive ointment ought to have been sold and the money given to the poor.

"And Jesus said, Let her alone; why trouble ye her? she hath wrought a good work on me. For ye have the poor with you always, and whensoever ye will ye may do them good: but me ye have not always. She hath done what she could: she is come aforehand to anoint my body to the burying. Verily I say unto you, Wheresoever this gospel shall be preached throughout the whole world, this also that she hath done shall be spoken of for a memorial of her."—Mark 14:6-9.

In the famous Museum at Cairo, the guide showed us an alabaster vessel which came from the tomb of Pharaoh Tutankhamen. It had contained sweet perfume, was sealed, and the guide said when it was opened the odor was still discernible.

Oh, it was an expensive and precious gift that Mary brought to anoint Jesus. How pleased was the Saviour over it!

These things happened on the Mount of Olives in the village of Bethany, just east of Jerusalem. And they helped to make the Mount of Olives precious to us.

II. IT WAS FROM THE MOUNT OF OLIVES THAT JESUS MADE THE TRIUMPHAL ENTRY INTO JERUSALEM

The last time Jesus approached Jerusalem He came from Galilee down the River Jordan to Jericho, then up the hill from the east, and so He came first to the Mount of Olives and then to the city.

1. It Was Foretold That Christ Would Come Lowly, Riding Upon an Ass Into Jerusalem

That prophecy was given in Zechariah 9:9: "Rejoice greatly, O daughter of Zion; shout, O daughter of Jerusalem: behold, thy King cometh unto thee: he is just, and having salvation; lowly, and riding upon an ass, and upon a colt the foal of an ass."

No doubt Jesus, who sometimes came down through Samaria and came in from the north, now deliberately chose to come this way to fulfill the prophecy. How carefully Jesus always did things that the "word of the Lord. . .might be fulfilled" (Ezra 1:1; John 19:24,28,36).

So when He came to the Mount of Olives, "He saith unto them, Go your way into the village over against you: and as soon as ye be entered into it, ye shall find a colt tied, whereon never man sat; loose him, and bring him." They were instructed to say, ". . .that the Lord hath need of him. . . ." The Master sent them along for the donkey and the donkey colt. They brought them to Jesus and they put their garments on the colt and Jesus sat on him.

"And many spread their garments in the way: and others cut down branches off the trees, and strawed them in the way. And they that went before, and they that followed, cried, saying, Hosanna; Blessed is he that cometh in the name of the Lord: Blessed be the kingdom of our father David, that cometh in the name of the Lord: Hosanna in the highest. And Jesus entered into Jerusalem, and into the temple: and when he had looked round about upon all things, and now the eventide was come, he went out unto Bethany with the twelve."—See Mark 11:1-11.

Oh, how the multitude cried out, "Blessed be the King that cometh in the name of the Lord: peace in heaven, and glory in

the highest." But when the Pharisees insisted Jesus should rebuke the disciples, He said, "I tell you that, if these should hold their peace, the stones would immediately cry out" (Luke 19:38-40).

I walked with holy joy down the trail, surely near the same trail where Jesus walked down the Mount of Olives, crossed the Brook Kidron or Cedron, and up into the old city of Jerusalem on His triumphal entry.

Called Chapel of Ascension on Mount of Olives

2. It Was Here That Jesus Stopped on the Mount of Olives and Wept Over Jerusalem

In Luke 19:37 we read that it was on this Mount of Olives when the disciples began to praise the Lord ". . .for all the mighty works that they had seen." Then in verses 41 to 44 we find Jesus weeping over the city.

"And when he was come near, he beheld the city, and wept over it, Saying, If thou hadst known, even thou, at least in this thy day, the things which belong unto thy peace! but now they are hid from thine eyes. For the days shall come upon thee, that thine enemies shall cast a trench about thee, and compass thee round, and keep thee in on every side, And shall lay thee even with the ground, and thy children within thee; and they shall not leave in thee one stone upon another; because thou knewest not the time of thy visitation."

In Matthew 23:37-39, this lament is given also.

See Jesus here,

> **Weeping, weeping o'er the city**
> **On the Mount of Olives Jesus stood**
> **Grieving o'er His sore rejection**
> **And the doom impending**
> **On the city loved so well.**

Or as the sweet ancient song:

> **The Son of God in tears**
> **And shall my tears be dry?**
> **Let tears of penitential grief**
> **Flow forth from every eye.**

Jesus had had a broken heart over Jerusalem a long time. Before this, when He was journeying toward Jerusalem and people had warned Him that He had better flee away lest Herod should kill Him, He said, "Nevertheless I must walk to day, and to morrow, and the day following: for it cannot be that a prophet perish out of Jerusalem."

"And he said unto them, Go ye, and tell that fox, Behold, I cast out devils, and I do cures to day and to morrow, and the third day I shall be perfected. Nevertheless I must walk to day, and to morrow, and the day following: for it cannot be that a prophet perish out of Jerusalem. O Jerusalem, Jerusalem, which killest the prophets, and stonest them that are sent unto thee; how often would I have gathered thy children together, as a hen doth gather her brood under her wings, and ye would not!

Behold, your house is left unto you desolate: and verily I say unto you, Ye shall not see me, until the time come when ye shall say, Blessed is he that cometh in the name of the Lord."—Luke 13:32-35.

Oh, the compassion of our Saviour toward that great city, the city of God, so filled with rebellious people and careless, but dear to the Lord!

The Mount of Olives is dear to us because it was dear to Jesus, and it was the site of many of His experiences near and around Jerusalem.

III. ON THE MOUNT OF OLIVES JESUS GAVE, FOR THE LAST TIME, HIS GREAT COMMISSION

It is true that the Garden of Gethsemane is on the cityward slope of Mount of Olives, and there Jesus loved to go, but we will deal with that in another message.

1. Jesus Gave the Great Commission Five Times in the Forty Days After His Resurrection

Once it was in the province of Galilee where Jesus had agreed to meet with the disciples.

"And Jesus came and spake unto them, saying, All power is given unto me in heaven and in earth. Go ye therefore, and teach all nations, baptizing them in the name of the Father, and of the Son, and of the Holy Ghost: Teaching them to observe all things whatsoever I have commanded you: and, lo, I am with you alway, even unto the end of the world. Amen."—Matt. 28:18-20.

Another time, probably the day of the resurrection, Jesus appeared to the eleven as they sat at meat.

"Afterward he appeared unto the eleven as they sat at meat, and upbraided them with their unbelief and hardness of heart, because they believed not them which had seen him after he was risen. And he said unto them, Go ye into all the world, and preach the gospel to every creature. He that believeth and is baptized shall be saved; but he that believeth not shall be damned."—Mark 16:14-16.

The statement of the Great Commission, perhaps the same occasion, is recorded in Luke 24:46-49. And they were commanded, "Tarry ye in the city of Jerusalem until ye be endued with power from on high."

The same day Jesus rose from the dead, at evening He appeared unto the disciples and said, "Peace be unto you: as my Father hath sent me, even so send I you. And when he had said this, he breathed on them, and saith unto them, Receive ye the Holy Ghost" (John 20:21,22).

Then the Great Commission is repeated in the first chapter of Acts. This, we think, is a resume of the statement from Luke 24. He told them not to depart from Jerusalem but wait for the promise of the Father: "But ye shall receive power, after that the Holy Ghost is come upon you: and ye shall be witnesses unto me both in Jerusalem, and in all Judaea, and in Samaria, and unto the uttermost part of the earth" (Acts 1:8).

2. The Great Commission Was Very Explicit

First, it was for everybody. Those who were saved were to be baptized and taught to carry out the Great Commission in Matthew 28:20. The Commission was to go to every person in the world, every creature. "And he said unto them, Go ye into all the world, and preach the gospel to every creature" (Mark 16:15). Then the disciples were clearly taught they must tarry for the power of the Holy Spirit.

These are the final instructions of the Saviour. How urgently He put it upon the heart of every Christian to win souls. If these disciples are to win souls, so are we. We are bought with the same blood as they are. We have the same Great Commission. If they were sent like Jesus was sent, so are we. If they were the "light of the world," so are we. And Revelation 22:17 plainly says, "Let him that heareth say, Come."

The business of Christ is saving sinners. The business of Christians is the same business—saving sinners.

Years ago Dr. John R. Sampey, president of the Southern Baptist Seminary at Louisville, Kentucky, and president of the Southern Baptist Convention, wrote, "The Gospel Train runs on two rails—education and evangelism." But he was wrong. The Gospel Train itself is evangelism.

Years ago when I was field secretary for Wayland Baptist College at Plainview, Texas, I sometimes preached from the Great Commission in Matthew 28:19,20, that we were to make disciples and then teach them, and I said, "Win souls and give them an education." I was boosting college education. But I was wrong. Christian education is a means, not an end. A Christian school has an excuse for being if it trains soul winners and helps carry out this Great Commission. Otherwise, it is secular and not Christian. Any work that is not someway covered by this Great Commission misses the one thing dearest to the heart of God, misses the one thing He plainly instructed every Christian to have in heart and to work at. Christians are to win souls.

IV. CHRIST ASCENDED TO HEAVEN FROM THE MOUNT OF OLIVES

It seems clear that the last time Jesus gave the Great Commission to the disciples was when they were assembled on the Mount of Olives itself. And it was there He ascended.

1. They Saw Him Go Up, Up, Up, Until a Cloud Received Him Out of Their Sight

Acts 1:9-12 says:

"And when he had spoken these things, while they beheld, he was taken up; and a cloud received him out of their sight. And while they looked stedfastly toward heaven as he went up, behold, two men stood by them in white apparel; Which also said, Ye men of Galilee, why stand ye gazing up into heaven? this same Jesus, which is taken up from you into heaven, shall so come in like manner as ye have seen him go into heaven. Then returned they unto Jerusalem from the mount called Olivet, which is from Jerusalem a sabbath day's journey."

The Saviour had been with the disciples forty days. "To whom also he shewed himself alive after his passion by many infallible proofs, being seen of them forty days, and speaking of the things pertaining to the kingdom of God" (Acts 1:3). We suppose that in one place and then another, again and again, to one group and then to another group and to as many as five hundred at one time

(I Cor. 15:6), Jesus had showed Himself to the disciples. He had eaten before them, their hands had handled Him. They had heard Him speak and rejoiced in His fellowship. The proof was infallible.

But now, it is not that He will slip away to appear to them again. It is an obvious, public leaving of His earthly ministry. And so He goes up, up, and a cloud receives Him out of their sight.

It was a cloud that covered Him on the Mount of Transfiguration when He was in His glory and when Moses and Elijah appeared to Him, and then He was covered. And then the outward glory disappeared and He went down the Mount of Transfiguration to the disciples and the troubled multitude below.

2. Angels Announce Christ's Second Coming

The return mentioned here is not that phase of the return which we think of as the rapture, when Christ will call all of His own out to meet Him in the air and the dead in Christ shall rise and the living shall be changed and meet the Lord and go away to the honeymoon in Heaven and the judgment seat of Christ, while this earth is troubled in Daniel's seventieth week in the last three and one half years that make the Great Tribulation. No, this is the literal, visible, bodily return of Christ to reign, when He comes back to set up His kingdom on earth.

Notice the angel said that He "shall so come in like manner." That means He will come with a literal, physical body like He went away, that body that ate and drank before them, that body their hands had handled. Christ will return.

He will come in the clouds of the air, because Revelation 1:7 says, "Behold, he cometh with clouds; and every eye shall see him, and they also which pierced him: and all kindreds of the earth shall wail because of him. Even so, Amen."

It was foretold ahead of time that "his feet shall stand in that day upon the mount of Olives, which is before Jerusalem on the east, and the mount of Olives shall cleave in the midst thereof toward the east and toward the west, and there shall be a very great valley; and half of the mountain shall remove toward the north, and half of it toward the south" (Zech. 14:4).

Catholic tradition has led to the building of a "Chapel of Ascension" on the Mount of Olives and there in a stone is a gigantic imprint a little like a bare foot, and they foolishly say that that was an imprint Jesus left when He ascended! In the first place, Jesus' foot was not that big, but was normal size. In the second place, there would be no reason for Him to leave a footprint. God does not want us worshiping places.

Ah, but praise the Lord for the sweet assurance that Jesus is coming again! The kingdoms of this world are not good. Satan is the god of this world. There is often injustice. There is crime, there is godlessness, there is sin. There is much to grieve the heart of a Christian in this world. But, thank God, Jesus Himself will return one day and His feet will touch the Mount of Olives. Then the Lord Jesus will put down all the kings of this world as is plainly foretold in Daniel, chapter 2, and pictured by a great stone cut out of a mountain without hand. And that stone in the dream of Nebuchadnezzar smote the image picturing the world empires, and ground it to powder and

**"Jesus shall reign where'er the sun
Does his successive journeys run."**

How dear to a Christian is this Mount of Olives! I rejoiced when I first saw it coming up from Jerusalem one day. I rejoice again when I walk up on it and remember that Jesus spent much time on this little hill or mount just across the little valley from old Jerusalem.

SWORD BOOKS

By Dr. Tom Malone, Sr. – a Truly Great Preacher!

MOUNTAIN PEAKS OF CHRIST

By Dr. Tom Malone. This author's sermonic material is rapidly gaining in popularity among preachers and lay people alike. In this volume Dr. Malone presents a glorious word picture of Christ—a panoramic view of His incomparable life and ministry from glory to glory. 9 chapters, 229 pages. **$3.50.**

ESSENTIALS OF EVANGELISM

By Dr. Tom Malone. 13 chapters, containing the Bob Jones University Lectures on Evangelism for 1958. Invaluable suggestions as to preparation for evangelistic meetings on the part of both the church or churches and the evangelist, church's obligation to the evangelist, and vice versa, etc. 166 pages, **$3.00.**

Sweet Psalms for God's Saints

Dr. Malone is a *heart* preacher and you will be borne along with one who confesses he has "sobbed with David, sung with the saints, and shouted with the blessed. . .walked through the green pastures, rested by the still waters and fellowshipped in the deep valleys." Psalms considered include Psalms 1, 22, 23, 24, 37, 40, 42, 43, 51, 61, 70, 91, 107, 119 and 137.

We urge you to get this book and discover why. 15 chapters, 341 pages, **$5.50.**

Postage and handling rates: up to $5.00, 35¢; over $5.00, add 7%. Tenn. residents please add 6% sales tax.

SWORD OF THE LORD Murfreesboro, Tennessee 37130.

★★★★★ **Learn How to Pray!** ★★★★★

PRAYER—

Asking and Receiving

$4²⁵

By Dr. John R. Rice. Dr. Rice drives home to the heart of every reader that prayer is asking for something from God and the answer to that prayer is receiving what you ask for. Who should pray? How should you pray? When should you pray? Will God really answer my prayer? These and many other questions are answered in this big 328-page book. 21 chapters that will teach you to pray and you too can start having your prayers answered. A book that you will cherish! (Also paperbound—**$1.95**.)

Whosoever and Whatsoever
WHEN YOU PRAY
$3⁵⁰

By Dr. John R. Rice. The author's life has been one of an endless succession of thrilling experiences in answered prayer. Illustrations of this fact, together with additional valuable lessons learned in the school of prayer, go to make up this latest volume on this subject of universal interest among Christians—and among many unsaved people, too! 9 chapters, fresh, new teaching on prayer—a worthy sequel to the author's original work on the same subject. 188 pages.

FILL MY CUP, LORD!
$4⁷⁵

By Jessie Rice Sandberg, being more "conversations with Christian wives and mothers," a worthy sequel in the high-quality literary tradition of the author's original work of its kind, *From My Kitchen Window.* This larger volume of 333 pages, regular library binding, contains 128 brief, inspirational, spiritual essays, being take-offs from routine incidents and personal contacts largely peculiar to the author and/or members of her exemplary family.

Postage and handling rates: up to $5.00, 35¢; over $5.00, add 7%. Tenn. residents please add 6% sales tax.
SWORD OF THE LORD   Murfreesboro, Tennessee 37130.

Inspirational!
Convicting!
Practical!

742 HEART-WARMING POEMS

Compiled. Contains many of Dr. Rice's own poems along with those by the best Christian and classical poets such as Shakespeare, Wordsworth, Tennyson, Crosby, Flint, Havergal, and others. Other contemporary writers are Bill Harvey and L. O. Engelmann. Poems are grouped under different topics; also carefully indexed as to authors, titles and first lines. 333 large pages. **$5.95**

"DO RIGHT!"

By the late Dr. Bob Jones, Sr. A rich, spiritual legacy has been left by this "giant of the faith" in this volume of 16 of his best messages. Note some of the chapter titles: "Do Right Though the Stars Fall," "'Rabbit Chasers,'" "Leaving All for Jesus," "Cooperating for Soul Winning," "Lot, the Compromiser," and "Where Are We Headed?" Every preacher and ministerial student should ponder these sermons. 317 pages. **$5.95**

THE HYLES SUNDAY SCHOOL MANUAL

By Dr. Jack Hyles. This is Volume II in the Hyles Manual Series. A comprehensive blueprint for building a large soul-winning Sunday school, combining the wisdom of the sages from the Sacred Pages with tried-and-proven methods of a modern-day, eminently successful Sunday school staff and organization, the First Baptist Church Sunday School of Hammond, Indiana. Another large volume, 256 pages. **$5.50**

Postage and handling rates: up to $5.00, 35¢; over $5.00, add 7%. Tenn. residents please add 6% sales tax.
SWORD OF THE LORD   Murfreesboro, Tennessee 37130.